STOP
CHASING
PROSPECTS

A Simple, 5-Step Formula
To Help You Quickly Establish Trust, Confidence,
And a Powerful, Authority Position
So Prospects Chase You

WESTON LYON

Copyright © 2018, Weston Lyon.

All rights reserved.

No part of this book may be reproduced or transmitted in any form or by any means, electronic or mechanical, including photocopying, recording, or by any information retrieval system, without permission in writing from the publisher.

Writing & Publishing Process by PlugAndPlayPublishing.com
Book Cover by Tracey Miller | TraceOfStyle.com
Edited by Jenny Butterfield

ISBN-13: 978-1986317443
ISBN-10: 1986317447

Disclaimer: This book contains opinions, ideas, experiences, and exercises. The purchaser and/or reader of these materials assumes all responsibility for the use of this information. Weston Lyon, Weston Lyon Enterprises, and Publisher assume no responsibility and/or liability whatsoever for any purchaser and/or reader of these materials.

I dedicate this book to sugar maven, Jenny Butterfield. Without you this past year, I don't know how I would have survived. Thank you for being you, and thank you for your love and support. I love you more than the number of stars in our multiverse!

Table of Contents

Read This First	**1**
Chapter 1: How to Become a Real Authority	9
Chapter 2: 3 Ways to Speed Up the Learning Process	13
Chapter 3: How to Become Seen as an Authority	19
Chapter 4: Prospects Have Expectations	25
STEP 1 Be Relevant	**31**
Chapter 5: Situations, Circumstances, and Frame of Mind	35
Chapter 6: The Two Forces that Drive Us All	39
Chapter 7: The Ranking System in Your Brain	43
Chapter 8: The Raw Emotions That Motivate People to Act	47
STEP 2 Be Interesting	**51**
Chapter 9: Types of Authorities	55
Chapter 10: You Don't Have to Settle on Just One Type of Authority to Model	61
Chapter 11: Your Authority Character	65
Chapter 12: Your 3-Sentence Story	73

Chapter 13: Your Character's Qualities & Tendencies	77
Chapter 14: Your Character's Philosophy	83
STEP 3 Be Authority-Present	**89**
Chapter 15: Writing a Book	95
Chapter 16: Speaking on Stage	103
Chapter 17: 6 Steps to Giving an Unforgettable Speech	113
Chapter 18: Getting Into the Media	131
Chapter 19: Writing Your Press Release	147
Chapter 20: Leveraging Your Authority	155
STEP 4 Be Talkable	**175**
Chapter 21: Demonstrating Your Authority with Testimonials and Endorsements	179
Chapter 22: How to Get More Testimonials and Endorsements	187
Chapter 23: The Best Type of Referrals	195
Chapter 24: Make the Referral Giving Process Easy and Pleasurable	201
STEP 5 Be Undeniable	**213**
Chapter 25: How Others See You	217
Chapter 26: How You See Yourself	231
Your Next Steps…	239
About the Author	243
Are You Looking for a Speaker for Your Next Entrepreneurial Event?	245

Read This First

Every entrepreneur I know – big or small, new or seasoned, struggling or successful – thinks about and focuses his attention on ONE, main challenge he faces in his business every single day: generating more leads and converting more sales.

After all, that's what our businesses are really about, right? Yes, we're in business to help and serve our clients. But without leads and sales, we have no business. Without leads and sales, we don't have enough money to survive.

So, if generating more leads and converting more sales is the main problem most business owners face today, how do we solve that problem?

Well, most entrepreneurs' answer is to track down more prospects and beat them into submission. I'm here to tell you that while that's an option… it's an annoying and ineffective option at best. We don't need to chase more business. Instead, we need to STOP CHASING PROSPECTS and get prospects to start chasing us.

How do we do that? The answer is simple. You must learn how to position yourself as a trusted authority.

What Is an Authority and Why Is Becoming an Authority the Answer?

An authority is someone who has power, knowledge, and expertise in his chosen field. Authority figures are seen as leaders. They are seen as people you can trust and people you can have confidence in.

That's why becoming an authority is important. In our society, people have trust and confidence in authority figures. What customers really want is to give their money to someone they can trust in exchange for the goods, services, and information that they are looking for.

Look, commerce is built on trust and confidence. Without trust and confidence, people won't buy. Fear will stop them dead in their tracks. However, by positioning yourself as an authority, you can establish trust and confidence faster and make sales easier.

Now, with that information in mind, we can use this fact to our advantage. No, we're not going to trick anyone. That would be wrong, unethical, and very uncool. However, we can use the fact that people trust authorities, buy with less resistance from authorities, and buy more from authorities to become an authority ourselves and reap the rewards.

How are we going to do this? First, we're going to look at what real authorities do and what people expect from experts. And then we're going to reverse engineer the process, so you can become an authority in your field.

By following the steps in this book, you can become an expert and authority in your field and grow your business with less resistance. Now, before we get started, there are a few things I want to cover with you:

Expectations

First, let me cover expectations. I'm going to lay out a plan for you to become an expert in your field. By following this plan, you can expect prospects to see you as an authority, and you can expect prospects to have less resistance in the buying stage. Meaning, you should fully expect to grow your business by using this book.

However, you should only expect those results if, and only IF, you follow the plan I lay out for you. There's no short cuts to success. Positioning yourself as an authority will take hard work and dedication. And that brings me to…

A BIG DISCLAIMER

Just because you are an expert in your field doesn't mean you'll have the financial success you desire. Yes, I've experienced financial success because of my authority position. Yes, some of my clients have had financial success because of their authority position. But not every expert (and certainly not every client) has experienced the financial success they wish for. There are just too many variables at play to guarantee your success, including timing, luck, mindset, implementation, and much more.

Therefore... I cannot guarantee your success. That's an expectation I cannot give you. But let's be honest, I think you already knew that. Running a business takes work and it takes risk. You know that, and I know that. That's why we're in business. That's why we're willing to work 60-80 hours a week for ourselves instead of 40 hours a week for someone else.

We know that work and risk are part of the game. But we also know that work and risk are worth the reward. Otherwise, we'd go get a job and stop the insanity that comes with running a business.

Listen, deep down, I don't think work or risk scare you. As an entrepreneur, the words "work" and "risk" are a part of your normal, everyday vocabulary. Those words have meaning to you. They do for me. Those words are a part of your DNA and make up who you are.

And as a business mentor of mine continually points out: what's the alternative? Think about that for a moment. What's the alternative to you staying in business and not becoming an expert and authority in your field?

> By positioning yourself as an authority, you can establish trust and confidence faster and make sales easier.

To help you really internalize this concept, let me ask you a question: five years from now, where will you and your business be if you DO NOT become an authority in your field? Will you be better or worse than you are today? Will you be making more sales or less sales with the same poor position you have today? How would that make you feel?

Would you feel sick and tired of spinning your wheels, not getting anywhere, and making the same money you're making today? Would you feel frustrated and fed up that prospects treat you the same way they do now, like a salesperson and not an expert? How would all this make you feel? Take a moment and really internalize those feelings.

Now, let's turn this around. Five years from now, where will you and your business be if you DO become an authority in your field? Will you be better or worse than you are today? Will you be making more sales or less sales positioned as an authority in your field? Will sales and referrals be easier or harder for you if you were positioned as an authority in your field? How would THAT make you feel?

Would you feel sick and tired, or would you feel excited and rejuvenated? Would you feel frustrated and fed up, or would you feel amazing and on top of the world? How would all THIS make you feel?

With your five-year future in mind, what alternative sounds better to you? Would you rather be seen as a salesperson, chasing prospects and getting little respect? Or... would you rather been seen as an authority in your field, having prospects chase you with their wallets out, money in hand, wanting to give you their money? If you're still with me, I know which path you'd prefer.

The third and final point I want to make before we move on is about...

Responsibility

Are you a Spider-Man fan? I am. And one of my favorite quotes from the Spider-Man movies comes from Uncle Ben: "With great power comes great responsibility."

In this book, you're going to learn some very powerful strategies and tactics on positioning and persuasion. Therefore, since you'll gain "great power" by reading and implementing these strategies and tactics, I believe you have the responsible to use these new powers for good. Meaning, you have the responsibility to treat your prospects and clients right. You have the responsibility to only provide quality products and services that work. And you have the responsibility to offer your prospects and clients quality products and services that will benefit them and not just your pocketbook.

If you do not have those intentions, then I'm going to ask you to put this book down and not read about the powerful strategies and tactics inside. I do not believe in unethical business practices and would prefer you don't read past this paragraph.

Now, I honestly don't think the majority of readers have bad intentions. I think most readers have good intentions and are willing to be responsible for their actions and their reputations. So if this is you, if you have good intentions and you're willing to take on "great responsibility" with your newfound powers, then I encourage you to read on, my friend, and use your powers to help your clients in every way you can.

Are you ready to get started? It's time to learn how you can take advantage of your own powerful authority position and grow your business this year and for decades to come.

1

How to Become a Real Authority

In this chapter, we're going to talk about becoming a real authority. Listen, perception IS reality. What people perceive to be true is real to them. So, let me ask you a question: do you think that you have to be a real authority to be seen as a real authority to your target market?

Interestingly enough, the answer is "no." You see, since what people perceive to be true is real to them, you do not have to be a real authority to be seen as such. You just have to behave like a real authority to be perceived and seen as the expert.

So, here's the thing, whether you are an authority right now or not, this book will show you how to be seen as an expert. I recommend becoming a real authority, and I'll show you some ways to speed up that process. But in the meantime, please understand that you don't have to be an authority right now.

By simply following the steps I'm going to show you in this book, you will start to become an expert in your field. And as your confidence grows, you will start to feel like an authority. This is where I want you to be. I don't want you to feel like a fake. I want you to feel like a real authority. You just don't have to feel like one yet. But you will.

Now, naturally, the best way to position yourself as an expert is to become a real authority on your topic. So, let's talk about your becoming a real authority.

Real authorities focus on mastery. They focus on and obsess over learning everything there is to know about a specific subject or topic. So, that's where you want to start. You want to learn all there is to know about your topic.

Let me suggest the following. If I were to start all over again, here's what I'd do:

- I'd read and/or listen to the top ten books in my industry.
- I'd choose the top five experts in my field and study them. I'd read their books, listen to their audio programs, and watch their videos on their websites or on YouTube.
- I'd also choose the top five trade associations and industry magazines in my field of expertise and study their content.

I feel the need to point out that to become a real authority, you will need different points of view. Don't study one expert's material and copy off of him or her. Instead, study many authorities' material and craft your own philosophy and ideas. Take a simple concept and make it completely yours. Or take a complicated topic and make it simple.

Again, mastery is the name of the game at this stage. To become a real authority, you have to focus on mastery and learning everything you can about your topic. Only then can you become a real authority.

Understandably, this path to mastery may seem a little overwhelming at first. Let me point out that you can't possibly study all this material this week or this month. But you can study all of this material over the next few years. So, please understand... becoming a real authority is a process.

And becoming a real authority is a never-ending process. Real authorities never stop learning. They never stop reading, watching, and listening to other experts in their field. Remember, they believe in and focus on mastery. To become a real authority, you will have to do the same.

> "Those people who develop the ability to continuously acquire new and better forms of knowledge that they can apply to their work and to their lives will be the movers and shakers in our society for the indefinite future."
>
> ~Brian Tracy

2

3 Ways to Speed Up the Learning Process

Now, if you're like me, you're always interested in ways to speed up the learning process. Here are three ways to do just that:

Summarize What You Learn

After learning something, whether you just completed a chapter in a book, read an article, watched a YouTube video, or listened to an audio CD, immediately write a "summary" of what you just learned.

Yes, it's like being back in school. But schools make you summarize content for a reason. Summarizing helps you learn faster.

Listen to Audio Books and Audio Programs in Your Car

I don't know about you, but I spend a lot of time in my car. By listening to audio programs in my car, I'm able to invest in my education and authority positioning instead of listening to music.

Yes, there are times when I think you should listen to music or relax in silence. It soothes the soul. However, if you're truly focused on mastery, taking advantage of this time when you can to learn something new or reaffirm what you already know is a smart move. This extra learning time adds up fast too. For example, if you spend just 30 minutes in your car each day listening to an audio book or program, at the end of just one year, you'll have listened to 182 hours of educational material. That's sixteen audio books per year!

Remember I said you should start reading the top ten books in your industry? With only 30 minutes per day in your car, you can knock out those ten books in as little as seven months!

Literally Speed Up Your Learning

Some video players now-a-days have a built-in speed control that allows you to increase the speed of the audio or video. So, if the video is ten minutes long and I increase the speed from 1.0 (normal speed) to 1.5 (one-and-a-half times the normal speed), I can finish a video in six minutes and 40 seconds.

Some people talk so slowly that you can literally double the speed of their video and hear them clear as day. Doubling the speed of a ten-minute video will allow you to finish the video in only five minutes.

Admittedly, this technique may take a little getting used to. And I may not recommend this tactic if you're brand new to your field and you're just getting started. At that beginner's stage, learning the material is more important than how much material you get through. However, I will tell you that once you get used to listening and learning at a higher speed, the higher rate saves you hours and hours each year. Plus, once you become a real authority and really know your stuff, this allows you to get more information into your subconscious mind at record speed!

Bonus Tips to Speed Your Learning Curve

Okay, if you're interested, I have two additional, ninja ways for you to increase your rate of learning and understanding. Most people won't do what I'm about to say. However, if you're serious about learning, understanding, and internalizing the information you're about to become a real authority on, then I suggest you give these next two tips some serious consideration.

First, after reading a blog post, an article, or a chapter in a book, literally rewrite the post, article, or chapter verbatim. That's right. Literally write out every single word the author wrote.

I know this sounds crazy. But it works. Writing out what you just read will not only help you learn the material faster, this technique will also help you internalize the author's language patterns.

Listen, the best authors have their own unique style of writing. They have a specific tone and voice in their writing. If you're going to become a real authority, then you have to find your own voice. Learning others' language patterns is a short cut to finding your own voice.

Just like I mentioned earlier, you don't want to study one authority and copy his material and ideas. You want to learn from a variety of authorities to round out your knowledge base and form your own opinions and ideas. The same is true for your tone and voice. Studying a variety of experts' language patterns will help you formulate your own language pattern faster.

By the way, the same is true for learning how to write anything better. If you want to learn to write fiction, rewrite your favorite fiction books. If you want to learn to write compelling sales copy, rewrite great sales letters, advisements, and website copy.

The second ninja way is to rewrite your own versions of what you learn. For example, if you read a great article, rewrite that article in your own words. Don't just write a summary of the article. Instead, write a full-blown article about the same subject you just read about.

This exercise will not only help you internalize the material, but it will help you find your own voice in the process. Down the road, as you find your own voice and get better at making content your own, you can use these articles for your own business.

But just to be clear: you're not plagiarizing anyone. You're writing a new article. Your own article with your own ideas. Yes, this new article is based on the other article you just read, but the content and the voice are yours and yours alone. Your content. Your voice. Your tone. Your language pattern.

Now, if you're thinking that these last two tips are tedious and take time, you're right. These two tips are tedious, and they do take time. But they are well worth the time you put in them.

Like I said, real authorities focus on and obsess over learning everything there is to know about their specific subject or topic. They know, understand, and even enjoy the process of mastering their craft and becoming the best at what they do.

Will you become a real authority in your field? I hope so. And I just gave you the road map to do just that in the shortest time possible.

In the next chapter, we'll look at how you can become *seen* as an authority.

3

How to Become *Seen* as an Authority

Okay, now that we know how to become a real authority, let's look at how to become SEEN as an authority. Like I mentioned before, you do not have to be a real authority to be seen as such. Remember, perception is reality. So, if you do what other authorities do and you behave how other authorities behave, then you'll be perceived as an authority. The majority of this chapter will focus on that fact.

But before we dive in, there's another truth I need you to be aware of first…

Just because you ARE a real authority on your topic doesn't mean your prospects SEE you as a real authority.

This is a trap many entrepreneurs fall into. Many entrepreneurs get upset and frustrated that their prospects buy from their competitors even though these entrepreneurs are the

> To be seen as an authority, you have to demonstrate your authority.

best in their fields and their competitors don't even come close.

I get it. If you're the best at what you do, then you should have a line of prospects waiting to hand you money because you can help them get the results they desire.

But unfortunately, that's not how the world works. Prospects buy from the people they know, like, and trust. They buy from the people they believe and perceive to be experts.

So, if we're not going to fall victim to this deadly trap, we have to understand that success isn't just based on our expertise. Success is based on how prospects perceive us.

To be seen as an authority, you have to demonstrate your authority. That's what we'll cover in the rest of this book: five ways to demonstrate your authority so your prospects see you as a real authority, have trust and confidence in you and your ability to help them, and buy from you and not your competition.

Now, like I mentioned earlier, I believe you should become a real authority. You should master your craft and focus on mastery in all that you do. But since perception is reality, you don't have to be a real authority yet. The key word being "yet." Instead, our prospects can see us as authorities as we study and grow into the real authorities we are destined to be. How?

We can manufacture an authority position by reversing engineering how people see authorities and what prospects expect from authorities. Then we can model that behavior to be seen as authorities in our prospects' minds.

A Moment on Ethics

"But, Weston, is positioning yourself as an authority, even though you're not an authority, ethical?" I get this question a lot, and the answer is not black and white. The real answer is in the grey area, and like any question on ethics, your personal answer to this question depends on your intent.

So, if you're a charlatan who is manipulating people into believing that you're an authority and getting them to buy from you, even though you offer no value, you can't genuinely help your clients, and you're just in it for the money… Then "yes," you're a no-good crook, and what you're doing is unethical.

I don't like these people, and I'd beat them with an ugly-stick if I wouldn't go to jail for it. They're a blight on society and give the rest of us good, helpful, honest entrepreneurs a bad name. They should be stopped and punished! They're crooks and thieves.

However, if you're a good, honest, helpful entrepreneur who is in the process of mastering your craft, becoming a real authority, and can add real, actual value to your clientele… Then "no," you're not being unethical. Your intent is good, and it's only a matter of time and education before you're a real authority.

Okay, I'll get down off my soapbox, so we can continue our conversation on how you can become seen as an authority. In the next chapter, we'll look at the expectations prospects have about authorities and why becoming a real authority is critical to your success.

4

Prospects Have Expectations

Prospects have expectations about what authorities do, how they behave, and what they look like. So, we need to first look at these expectations and then learn how to adopt an authority's mindset and an authority's behavior.

What Do Authorities Believe?

- Authorities believe in mastery in their field of study. They believe in studying and remaining curious. They believe in educating their audience with useful information.

- Authorities believe in having their own ideas and their own perspective. They believe in themselves and their ideas, and they are not afraid to disagree with other experts in their field.

- Authorities believe in and are willing to take calculated risks because of their confidence in their own abilities. They believe in excellence, not perfection. They embrace their mistakes and move on quickly.

What Do Authorities Do?

- Authorities have read, listened, and learned from the other greats in their industry. They have internalized that information and have a deep understanding of their topic.

- Authorities are self-aware of their performance and can correct themselves. They have a knack for doing what they do because they are unconsciously competent in their craft, meaning that their craft is so internalized that they could probably perform in their sleep.

- Authorities continue to constantly learn and grow. They appear in the media. They charge more than most in their field because they are sought after and have limited time.

- Authorities are not afraid to turn business away. They are in charge and don't back down on their ideas. They don't appease people or cave in. They have resolve.

- Authorities are not afraid to be out in front and leading people. They prescribe solutions, and they do not beg or sell from a poor position. They come from a position of power.

> "The wrong mindset will hold you back. The right mindset will set you free."

- Authorities have people talking about them: both good and bad. And they're not afraid of criticism. They dress the part, and they know how to relate to their target audience.

- Authorities know what their target audience wants, how their prospects feel, and they care about their audience. They tend to simplify complex concepts in their own way, and they share those new concepts with their audience.

I'm sure we could come up with more examples of what authorities believe and how they behave, but I think you get the gist.

So, why did we look at this list of actions and beliefs? Because you are what you think about and do on a consistent basis. To be a real authority and to be seen as a real authority, you have to believe and do what real authorities believe and do.

Remember what I said, "what people perceive is real to them." The same is true for you. What you perceive is real to you. So, if you perceive yourself as an authority, then you'll act like an authority. And if you act like an authority, then you'll be seen and treated like an authority.

To some people, this approach may seem a little too far-fetched or outrageous. However, I encourage you to re-read the list of beliefs, actions, and behaviors above because getting into an authority mindset can be the difference between you being seen as an authority or being seen as a fake.

And having an authority mindset can be the difference between you becoming a real authority or staying where you are.

Your mindset has everything to do with whether or not you'll be successful. The wrong mindset will hold you back. The right mindset will set you free. Free to become who you are meant to become. Free to serve and help who you are meant to serve.

This is the beginning of getting your head straight and getting into an authority mindset. We'll cover a more practical/applicable way of doing this later on in this book, but for now, please understand that this mindset step is critical to your success as an expert and authority in your field.

The rest of this book is dedicated to showing you what authorities do, how they behave, and how you can model their actions to be seen as an authority – whether you are a real authority or you're on your way to becoming one.

BE RELEVANT

Some experts will try to get you to believe that positioning yourself as an authority will take years (it won't) or that there is some mystical secret behind having expert status (there's not).

In truth, there are only five main factors you need to know to demonstrate your authority:

1. What you say,
2. How you say it,
3. Where you say it,
4. What others say about you, and
5. How others see you.

In this chapter, we'll begin to look at the first factor: what you say.

People are quick to judge. When we hear someone speak for the first time, we make a decision within the first few seconds as to whether we will:

a) really listen to him,
b) hear him out just to be nice, or
c) ignore him completely.

That's why the message you communicate (what you say) must be relevant, interesting, and unique.

Let's look at relevancy first. Our brains are always looking for relevancy. If your message isn't relevant, then people cannot help but ignore you. That's why choosing the right target market is so important. The right market will find your message relevant, and they will pay attention to you. The wrong market will find your message irrelevant, and they will ignore your message without giving you much thought.

These people aren't trying to be rude to you. Their non-interest has nothing to do with you. They're ignoring you simply because your MESSAGE isn't relevant, and their brains choose to ignore the message, not you.

Think about yourself for a second. When you flip through a magazine, do you read every article and advertisement? Of course not! Why? Because the majority of the articles and ads aren't relevant to you!

For example, if you're a man, the chance that an article on how to apply makeup for a sexy night on the town or an ad on which makeup is best for your skin is probably not relevant to you. Oh, I know, there's a chance (and I'm not judging), but I think you can agree with me that a man being concerned about makeup is rarer than a woman being concerned about the same topic. That same magazine is more relevant to a female audience.

The same concept not only applies to magazines but to any media with any audience. For instance, I'm a mountain biker. When I scroll through my YouTube feed, do you think I stop to investigate a video about mountain biking? You bet I do. Why? Because it's relevant to me. If you're a mountain biker, then you'd stop to look at the video too. Now, you may not watch the entire video, but you'd at least check out the title and maybe watch the first minute. Then, if the content is interesting to you (which we'll cover next), you'll watch the entire video. However, if you're not a mountain biker, you probably wouldn't even give that video the time of day. Again, if the information is not relevant to you, it wouldn't even pop up on your mental radar.

Relevancy is the first key to your message being looked at, watched, and listened to. So, if that's the case, then how do you make your message more relevant?

First, you must figure out what situations your target audience is experiencing. Then, you have to understand what drives them and what they value. Finally, you have to communicate that you have a solution to help them conquer their fears, achieve their desires, and move toward their ideal situation.

5

Situations, Circumstances, and Frame of Mind

The first step to making sure your message is relevant is to figure out what situations your target audience is experiencing and going through right now. Some situations are positive, while some are negative. Let's look at several examples for both types of situations that three different target markets might experience.

If your target market includes business owners, like mine does, *some negative situations your prospects may be going through right now may include:*

- Not generating enough leads
- Getting leads but not making many sales
- Getting sales but not making much profit

Some positive situations may include:

- Growing so fast they have to hire someone to help them keep up
- Making more money than ever before and needing to know about investment allocation and tax havens

If your target market includes new parents, then *a few negative situations they may be experiencing right now may include:*

- Sleepless nights
- Intrusive and overbearing grandparents
- Not getting enough alone time or adult interaction

Some positive situations may include:

- Understanding and time-generous grandparents
- Experiencing complete joy and happiness with their baby and/or their new family

If your target market includes divorced housewives, then *a few negative situations they may be going through right now may include:*

- Feeling alone and depressed
- Experiencing money problems
- Selling a home and splitting their assets

Some positive situations may include:

- Finally getting rid of their cheating, no-good husband
- Leaving a stale or dying marriage for a brighter, more vibrant future

As you can see, there are two sides to every coin. People can view the same situation in two different ways depending on their frame of mind. For example, a divorced housewife can end up feeling alone and depressed or excited about her new future.

Everyone is different in how he processes the situations he experiences. His attitude and reaction are based on what drives him and what he values (which we'll explore next).

Before moving on, think about and jot down some situations your ideal, target market is most likely experiencing right now.

"Your message must be relevant, interesting, and unique."

6

The Two Forces that Drive Us All

Now that you know what situations your target audience is experiencing, let's look at what drives your prospects to take action. There are two types of forces that drive us all: pain and pleasure.

We all want to move towards things that we desire, things that cause us pleasure, happiness, joy, and ecstasy. At the same time, we all want to move away from things that we fear or things that cause us pain, sadness, suffering, and misery.

The question now becomes, "What drives your prospects the most?" What desires do they have, and what fears do they have? What do they want the most, and what do they run from? Let's continue with our previous examples…

If your target market includes business owners, then *some desires may include:*

- Making more sales and earning more money
- Having more time and freedom
- Growing a solid business that helps thousands, hundreds of thousands, or millions of people
- Making a difference in their community or their profession

Some fears they have may include:

- Not having enough money to survive
- Not having enough predictable income to get ahead
- Going (or going back) to work for someone else
- Appearing as hype-y or just another salesperson

If your target market includes new parents, then *some desires may include:*

- Being the best parents they can be
- Providing financial security for their family
- Staying home and not going back to work

Some fears they have may include:

- Having their baby get sick or injured
- Having to leave their baby with a sitter or at daycare
- Not being able to send their new child to college

If your target market includes divorced housewives, then *some desires may include:*

- Sticking it to their husbands
- Getting back together and making the marriage work
- Surviving on their own and making life go on

Some fears they have may include:

- Going back to work after years out of the workforce
- Running into unsupportive friends or frenemies
- Finding someone new after years, maybe decades, out of the dating scene

Okay, it's your turn. What do you think drives your prospects to take action? Make some mental notes before moving to the next chapter.

7

The Ranking System in Your Brain

Okay, so now you know the situations your target audience is going through, what they are trying to avoid (i.e. their fears), and what they are trying to achieve (i.e. their desires). Now, let's look at your prospects value system.

Our value system is a ranking system in our brains. Let me ask you a question. Out of these two drivers, which is more important to you: Freedom or Security?

For me, I rank Freedom over Security. Most entrepreneurs do. Knowing this information about your audience can help you talk to them about what's important to them. And talking to your audience about what's important to them allows you and your message to grab their attention. After all, you're speaking their language now, and your message is relevant to them.

With this information in hand, let's look at the business owner example we've been using. Here's what we know about the business owners in our example:

1. They're not generating enough leads or sales.

2. They desire having more time and freedom.

3. They fear not making enough money to survive or have the freedom they desire.

4. They value freedom above all else.

Knowing this information allows us to start crafting a message that hits them right between the eyes. For example, based on the information we know about this target audience, do you think this headline will grab the audience's attention?

Finally, Learn How to Build a Predictable Sales System That Generates Leads Every Single Day, So You Can Enjoy the Freedom You've Always Dreamt About!

Of course, it will! This headline hits them right between the eyes by allowing them to get what they want, stay away from what they don't want, and offers them a solution to their current situation.

That's what you want your message to do. And this message is what you want to represent to your ideal audience. You're the authority. You can help them. You can help them get out of their current situation and transition into the place they want to be.

But you can't do all this unless you know what drives your audiences and what your audience values most.

So, take a moment now and jot down some ideas about what you think your audience values most. Do they value freedom or security? Love or adventure? Beauty or grace? Power or intelligence? Immediacy or legacy? Honesty or righteousness? Forgiveness or compassion? Peace or prosperity?

And don't just think about positive values. Think about negative values too. Which drivers are of least value to your audience. Embarrassment or exclusion? Deceit or disrespectfulness? Injustice or dishonesty?

Also, there may be times when your audience values both drivers you pair together. That's good. You can use that quirk. But try to put yourself in their shoes, and think about what they want more. The more you know about your target audience's value system, the more powerful and relevant you can make your message and your authority.

8

The Raw Emotions That Motivate People to Act

Okay, you know the situations your target audience is going through, what they are trying to avoid (i.e. their fears), what they are trying to achieve (i.e. their desires), and what they value most. This is vital information for grabbing your audience's attention and staying relevant in their minds.

Now, let's look at your prospects' motives. Motives are the reasons why we move towards pleasure and away from pain. Motivations are the underlying reasons of any big "why," the raw emotions behind why you value what you value and why you do what you do.

For example, most entrepreneurs desire freedom above all else. But why? What are their underlying reasons? What are the emotions that cause their desire, fear, and behavior? While I can't answer this question for all entrepreneurs, I can tell you that the reason I desire freedom above most other drivers is because freedom allows me to do what I want, when I want, with whom I want. I don't like taking orders from other people. I don't like being at work at a specific time. I like making my own rules, and I enjoy working my own hours. Some may call that unruly or childish. But those people's opinion doesn't matter to me. I know what I want and why I want it.

I'm sure you feel the same way. Maybe not about freedom but about something else. You most likely have a gut reaction about something in your life. All people do. Our goal is to figure out what that "gut reaction" is for our audience.

So, what about the new parent? Again, I can't speak for all new parents, but I can tell you that when I was a new parent I valued my son's safety above all else. Why? Because my son was my entire world, and I didn't want anything to happen to him. That was my motive, and that deep-seeded emotion drove me to be the parent I was. Some may have called me a helicopter dad because I was always around, looking after him, making sure he didn't fall in the wrong spot. But my motive was clear. Protect my son at all costs.

Personally, I think that's just good parenting. But that's my opinion. You may have a different view point. I'm okay with that. But if you were selling something to me at the time I was a new parent (or parents like me), then your best message to us would include the phrases, "safety above all else," "your child is your world," and "that's what good parents do."

What about our divorced housewife? What drives her, and what does she value most? Is she broken-hearted and looking for a solution to ease her pain and suffering? If so, and she values love above all else, your message better not include anything about "getting back at your husband" or "making him pay." Her mindset isn't there. She values love, and she may even think they have a shot at getting back together.

On the other hand, if the divorced housewives you cater to feel wronged by their husbands and want to "take him to the cleaners," then you should use that language. At the moment, their values may have shifted from love to vengeance, so you should use a message that resonates with their current emotional state.

Take a moment now and jot down the motives, reasons, and emotions your ideal, target audience feels or thinks, why they desire what they desire, fear what they fear, and value what they value.

The First Step

You now know the first step to demonstrating your authority: BE RELEVANT by talking to your ideal, target audience about the situations they're going through, the fears they are trying to avoid, the desires they are trying to achieve, the drivers they value most, and underlying emotions they use to avoid pain, gain pleasure, and transition from their current situation to a new, ideal situation.

Knowing all this information and communicating it to your ideal, target audience will not only help you grab their attention, this deep, knowing communication will help you stay relevant and keep their attention. At least for a little bit.

You see, being relevant is the first step to making your message powerful and compelling… but relevancy isn't the only ingredient to your message's success.

In the next section, we'll explore the second factor and the second step to demonstrating your authority and creating trust and confidence with your prospects.

BE INTERESTING

Like I said in the last chapter, relevancy isn't the only ingredient to your message's success. What you say must also be interesting and unique! If your message is relevant but not interesting, you'll hold the person's attention for a short period of time, and then you'll lose his attention to boredom or some sort of "shiny object." If your message is relevant but not unique, you'll get your audience's attention and maybe hold their attention for a period of time, but then you'll lose them because you sound like everyone else. On the other hand, if your message is relevant, interesting, and unique, you'll grab your audience's attention and hold their attention indefinitely. So, now the big question becomes:

> How do you keep your message interesting, and how do you make your message unique?

While being relevant was in "what you said," being interesting and unique is all in "how you say it." The best way to make your message interesting and unique is to *make yourself interesting and unique* to your audience. Listen, there is no one on this planet that is just like you. You are unique, and no one else can copy you.

So, by making yourself the main character, by making *you* the main difference between your solution and your competitors solution, you insulate your business from your competition and attract the best customers for you.

Keeping your message interesting comes down to how you say something. For instance, if you speak with a lot of enthusiasm and passion in your voice, people will pay attention. Passion is contagious and interesting to a lot of listeners. Another way to create interest is to truly care about the person you're talking to and trying to help. When people feel that you care about them, you'll make a connection, and they'll pay attention to you. Another important factor to creating interest with your message lies in your ability to be yourself and show off your personality. If you're opinionated, then be loud and proud. If you're emotional and sensitive, then wear your heart on your sleeve. Don't try to be these things for show. Be yourself.

The worst thing you can do is fake your personality. People will see through you, and they'll ignore you and your message. The second worst thing you can do is be vanilla, middle of the road, or wishy-washy. People don't respond to or get interested in flavorless messages.

People read, listen, and watch polarizing messages. For example, why do millions of people listen to Howard Stern? It's not because he's the funniest guy on earth. People listen to him because they never know what's going to come out of his mouth next.

Why do millions of people love (or at least love listening to) Bill O'Reilly and Rush Limbaugh? It's because they're opinionated, and their messages strike a chord with their audiences. They're far from middle of the road. They're all the way on one side of the road, yelling at the people who oppose them.

There's a fascinating thing about being polarizing too. Stern, O'Reilly, and Limbaugh all have more "haters" listening to their shows than actual fans. Why? Because, whether or not you agree with these guys or like them, they're interesting characters with interesting ideas, and they say things in interesting ways! Now, I'm not saying you have to be like these guys. That's not the point. The point is this…

You must be interesting. You must have something interesting to say. And you must learn to say things in your own, unique, interesting way.

To do all this, we first need to look into the future and see what type of authority you want to become and be recognized as. Then, we can reverse-engineer your Authority Position by creating your new and improved Authority Character.

> You must learn to say things in your own, unique, interesting way.

9

Types of Authorities

There are four main types of authorities you can become, which I've based on the four main types of **D&D** characters (at least the characters my buddies and I play with). If you're not familiar with **D&D**, it's short for **Dungeons and Dragons**, which is a fantasy role playing game (RPG, in case you want another nerdy acronym). **D&D** was created in 1970's and has a huge presence and following both online and offline. By the way, yes, I'm that big of a nerd. But, here's a fun fact: all modern-day RPG video games, like **World of Warcraft** and **Final Fantasy**, are based on **D&D**. So, while some people think **D&D** is a game for nerds (and it is), it's a game that has revolutionized game play for the past 45+ years.

Anyway, this isn't a lesson on the history of **D&D**. All you have to know is there are four main characters, and I've related those four main characters to the type of authority you can become. Here they are:

The Fighter

A Fighter is an authority who is in the trenches, fighting with you and showing you how he or she has done it. "Do this." "Don't step on that landmine." "Be careful of that trap." "You're home free, keep going!" Fighters don't have time for B.S. or shenanigans, so they typically don't pull any punches. Instead, they prefer to tell it you like it is whether you want to hear it or not. In addition, they are leaders who hate excuses. In fact, they aren't afraid to get their hands dirty, and they are willing to jump in and help you achieve your ultimate objective.

The perfect example of a Fighter Authority type is John McClain from the *Die Hard* movies. If you've never seen the *Die Hard* movies, stop reading this book and go watch them all right now! Okay, maybe not now, but soon. John McClain is a cop from New York who seems to find trouble everywhere he goes. From New York to L.A. to Russia, and everywhere in between. He's a take-no-prisoner type of guy (literally) and gets shit done. He has no problem telling you what to do or what he thinks about you. He doesn't "baby" anyone and is all about taking action to get the job done. He's a fighter.

The Mage

Unlike the Fighter, a Mage is an authority who doesn't necessarily enjoy the limelight. He or she can stand the heat of the spotlight and will get his hands dirty, but he typically prefer to stay back and help from a distance by taking an advisory role. In fact, think of the Mage as a reluctant hero. He is not necessarily in an authority role to be seen as an authority. A Mage is an authority because he feels obligated to show you how he's done something, so you can achieve the results you desire. Mages are typically a little more mild-mannered than the Fighter type too. Fighters are more abrasive. Mages are subtle and sophisticated. That doesn't mean mages cannot be abrasive or passionate. They can be. In fact, it's important to point out that each and every authority is a unique blend of one or two of these character types. Some authorities are a mix of all four types. The beauty of creating your own Authority Character is that you choose what people see and how they perceive you.

An example of a Mage Type is Morpheus from *The Matrix*. Morpheus is cool, calm, and collected. He's not afraid to fight for what he believes in, but his main objective is to help Neo, the main character, achieve his ultimate destiny. Morpheus is a general, comfortably sitting in the back seat, giving suggestions, and watching his protégé get all the glory.

The Healer

A Healer is an authority who is on a mission to search out and bring you the best possible information and solutions they can find. Like Fighters, Healers can be very opinionated and can be seen as crusaders who will stop at nothing to support you on your journey. Because Healers are so passionate about their cause, they tend to rub some people the wrong way. That's a good thing though because healers are able to move their cause forward faster by focusing on the people who want their help and by ignoring the people who are not ready for their particular brand of help. Healers are good people at heart and are very passionate. "Fanatical" may be a better term. But Healers have their fans and followers in mind at all times.

An example of a Healer Type is personal development guru, Tony Robbins. Tony has been helping people achieve their very best for over four decades now, and he packs more passion, drive, and energy in a single day than most people have in a lifetime. He's an inspiration and someone I love to listen to. Yes, he's opinionated. Yes, he's in your face with what he believes. But for those who enjoy his style and material, I feel he has your best interest at heart at all times. That's what makes him a Healer Type of authority.

The Rogue

A Rogue is an authority who "takes" other authorities' information and presents it to you in their own, unique way. They are reporters at heart and seek the truth about their area of expertise. Like Healers, Rogues are always in search of great content. They are natural learners, and they read and research a lot of books. They attend a lot of events. And they enjoy seeing what others are doing and learning. They then take that information, and they either report back to you with all their findings or they re-synthesize all that information with their own twist. Like Mages, and unlike Healers who can be evangelical, Rogues tend to keep to themselves and remain in the shadows.

The perfect example of a Rogue type is Captain Jack Sparrow from ***The Pirates of the Caribbean*** movies. Captain Jack seems to be everywhere and is always in the thick of things. He is an astute leader who always has his eyes and ears open for his next big score or opportunity. And while it may seem like you cannot trust this rogue, Jack AND his comrades always seem to get what they desire most. Also, even though the word "rogue" is related to "scoundrel" or "thief," the Rogue Authority, like Captain Jack's character, always has his fans and followers best interests at heart.

In the upcoming chapters, I'll walk you through a fun exercise to help you create your own Authority Character. But before I do, let's talk about an important aspect of your Authority Character…

10

You Don't Have to Settle on Just One Type of Authority to Model

You can blend specific traits together to create your own unique, Authority Character. In fact, that's what I'll encourage you to do because these authority types are not the end-all-be-all. They are not boxes to hold you back. Instead, they are meant to give you a place to start. Actually, to illustrate my point, let me give you two examples.

First, a fictitious example: you see, when I create a new *D&D* character, I first create the character's backstory. Where is he from? What struggles has he had in his life? What is he trying to achieve? In the upcoming chapters, we'll actually go through a similar exercise.

After I have his backstory, I then decide on the type of character he's going to be. Is he going to be a straight up Fighter who only enjoys the fighting and pillaging, or is he going to be a Fighter who can also heal himself and the rest of the party? Is he going to be a Mage who focuses on damage-producing magic, or is he going to be magic-user who deceives others with illusions and mind control just to steal their valuables? The combinations are endless, and playing around with what's right for the new character is a lot of fun.

Finally, I decide on how I'm going to play this character based on his backstory, the type of character he is (straight up Fighter vs. a Fighter/Healer vs. whatever combo I create), and how this character would react to outside forces (i.e. other characters, villains we come across, etc.).

The point is, no two characters are the same, and the type of characters I create are not solely based on the four, main character types. Each character is unique and possesses a blend of different traits, tendencies, and skill sets. Your Authority Character, the authority you want to become, is created in the same fashion. Again, we'll start down that path in the upcoming chapters.

Let me give you another example. This time a personal, real life example. When I think about my own personal Authority Character, I see myself as a Mage/Fighter (i.e. a Mage and a Fighter). I teach my clients how to position themselves as authorities in their fields, primarily by becoming authors, and then I show them how to leverage their authority to grow their businesses.

I'm extremely grateful for learning how to position myself as an authority at a time when I was broke and struggling. So, my Mage role tends to be one of the reluctant hero because I genuinely feel obligated to show you how to do what I've done, so you can reach your goals and dreams. I also don't mind standing in the background and not being the center of attention when it comes to your success. After all, I'm teaching you how to position yourself as your own authority so you can lead others.

At the same time, I like to play the role of a Fighter because it's more natural for me, and being in charge is part of who I am. That direct, in-your-face attitude has gotten me in trouble at times, but I do not apologize for making people uncomfortable when it's required for their growth. I try to tame that aspect of my Fighter side, but being a Fighter is a part of who I am, and I have found over the years that my clients come to me for that reason. I'm going to be nice and as sophisticated as I can be (the Mage side of me helps), but I am willing to tell it like it is and help you move forward by seeing through your excuses.

That actually brings me to one final point before we discuss creating your own, unique Authority Character. It's important to realize that…

You Shouldn't Change Who You Are

That would naïve and foolish. You have to be who you are. But that's not to say you can't become a better version of yourself. I think that's true for everyone, including those who are already seen as authorities in their fields. We're all trying to make ourselves better to better serve our clients. So, keep this idea in mind when you're creating your Authority Character: **You're not creating the character you are; you're creating the character you want to be.**

What's the best version of yourself? Who's the type of person you want to be seen as? That's the Authority Character you want to create and become. And if you're not that person yet, how can you become that person? It's a process. It's going to take time. But, by strategically creating the Authority Character you want to become, you can plan out and take the necessary steps you'll need to evolve and transform into that person.

Sometimes, just the simple act of creating your new character allows you to transform into that character because you're now able to identify what you have to do to become the person you're destined to become.

Okay, now we're ready to create the ideal, Authority Character that best reflects who you are, who you want to be, and who best serves your ideal, target audience.

11

Your Authority Character

It's time to start creating your Authority Character. To do so, we need to look at the three components of an Authority Character:

1. Your character's backstory
2. Your character's qualities and tendencies
3. Your character's philosophy

First, let's dive into...

Your Character's Backstory

Like any good story, your character's backstory is made up of three components:

1. Your struggle
2. Your transition
3. Your success

Think about most great movies you've seen. The main character goes through something – he or she goes through a struggle. He loses a friend, he gets injured, he goes through a breakup, etc. Then, something happens to allow the main character to transition out of the struggle. He sees a new way to live. A friend gives him a helping hand. He finds the true meaning of life. I don't know. Something happens, and he sees a better way. He transitions. Finally, he takes his newfound knowledge, experience, etc. and succeeds. Maybe he finds a new love. Maybe he grows wealthy. Maybe he quits his job and lives in pure bliss. He succeeds or wins in some way.

For example, I absolutely love the Marvel Cinematic Universe! I love all the characters, and I love how the writers have brilliantly weaved in all the story lines and plots to create amazing films. In the first **Iron Man** movie, Tony Stark is kidnapped by terrorists who have stolen his weapons of mass destruction and want him to build a missile for them. That's his struggle. Oh, and he has shrapnel in his chest that will kill him if he doesn't find a way to stop the little bits of metal from reaching his heart. Bottom line, he's in bad shape and under a lot of duress.

Then, with the help of a fellow captive, Tony builds an electromagnetic "arc reactor" to: a. keep the shrapnel at bay until he can escape, and b. power an armored suit that allows him to blow up the base and escape. That's the turning point of the movie. That's his transition.

Finally, after his horrible experience, Tony stops his company from creating weapons of mass destruction and turns his attention to creating a new type of weapon, the Iron Man suit, to protect the world instead of facilitating the destruction of mankind. The movie continues as he fights bad guys, finds out who's behind the big, evil plot, and ultimately saves the day in the end. That's his victory. His success.

While you may not be a billionaire, playboy, genius who saves the world, you have a backstory too. Something has happened in your past to make you the person you are. You've gone through some type of struggle. You've had an epiphany of sorts that made you transition. And you've succeeded in some way, big or small.

That's what we want to look at now. What's your backstory? Let's start this exercise by looking at…

Your Struggle

What are some things in your life that you have struggled with? If you're a fitness coach, were you a fat child or a lazy teenager who sat on the couch and ate Cheetos? Or maybe you enjoyed working out but couldn't find the right exercises for you to lose weight or gain muscle. Or maybe you got injured lifting weights and found a better way to get the same results.

In my past, business life, I was a fitness coach, and I built my business with a backstory like that. I injured my back lifting heavy weights in the gym at the young age of 23. I struggled

> You're not creating the character you are; you're creating the character you want to be.

with back pain and weight training until I found a better way.

Everyone has a story. Everyone has something he or she has struggled with, whether the struggle was mental, emotional, physical, or spiritual. How does your story begin? What struggles have you gone through? Or what struggles have you seen others go through to make you change your mindset about something?

Your struggle doesn't have to be something that happened to you directly. For example, maybe you're a business consultant who's always had success. But a theme you noticed was that all your clients were struggling with making more money or taking action because their mindset was off base. Instead of having an abundance mindset, they had a poverty mindset. You didn't struggle with anything. They did. Of course, please don't make any of this up. Be truthful and draw from your personal experience.

I think this exercise will come quite easily for you. However, if you need additional help please refer to Chapters 5 and 6, where we talk about your audience's situations and drivers. Be honest and think about the struggles in your life or the struggles you've seen in someone else's life that have led you to become the person and authority you are.

Your Transition

Now let's look at the moment your life changed, your transition. Like I said, in my fitness business I used the backstory of injuring my back lifting heavy weights in the gym and struggling with back pain and weight training until I found a better way. Again, that's a true story. That really happened.

I was then given a book by a friend of mine about the power of bodyweight training and how you can still get in shape without the dangers of training with heavy weights or free weights. That book opened my eyes to a whole other world. I was able to strengthen my back, especially the muscles that support the spine, and get back into the shape I was in without ever injuring myself that way again. This new way of training was a game changer for me. That was my transition. If the story stopped at my struggle, it wouldn't be much of a story, would it? The transition shows the audience the reason behind your success.

Let's take another Marvel movie and look at the transition. Have you ever seen *Captain America: The First Avenger*? Steve Rogers, a weak, sickly kid from Brooklyn with the heart of a lion, enlists in the army and is placed into an experimental program to create America's first super-soldier.

Steve's transition is when he's given the super-soldier serum. He enters the experiment chamber a scrawny kid, and then emerges from the chamber a man with bulging muscles and super-human strength.

As you can see, the transition doesn't have to be long or drawn out. In fact, the transition typically the shortest part of the back-story equation.

So, what was your transition? Did you read a book that changed your mindset? Did you meet a mentor or the love of your life? Did you see someone else struggle and decide to never let that happen to anyone else? Did you get injected with super-human strength serum, or were you bitten by a radioactive spider? Probably not, but you get the point. What was your transition point?

Your Success

Okay, now that you realize what your struggle and your transition was, let's look at your success. What success have you had since your transition point?

If we go back to my fitness business example, I injured my back in the weight room. I was then given a book on bodyweight training that allowed me to get back into shape without lifting weights. My success included getting in the best shape of my life without ever injuring my back again and without ever having to step into a gym again.

Tony Stark's success was when he built the Iron Man suit and saved the world. Steve Rogers success was when he became a super-solider with super-human strength and saved the world. In case you were wondering, most Marvel movies end with the same type of success, someone saving the world. And, yes, I'm comparing myself to super heroes. A boy can dream, can't he?

Anywho, what's your success entail? Did you go from broke and struggling to rich and living the life of your dreams? Did you go from being scared to talk to women to dating a supermodel? Did you go from being 100 pounds overweight to looking like Arnold Schwarzenegger? What's your success look like?

In the next chapter, we'll take these three pieces – your struggle, your transition, and your success – and we'll put them all together into a simple story.

12

Your 3-Sentence Story

Now that you have the raw material for your backstory, let's put all the pieces together into a simple story anyone can understand and pass along. Let's start by narrowing down your backstory to the bare essentials. Take your three components – your struggle, your transition, and your success – and write one sentence for each of them. For example, for my fitness coaching business, my simple story was:

Struggle: When I was 23 years old, I injured my back lifting weights and put myself out of commission for over a year.

Transition: Then, a friend of mine handed me a book that changed my life by teaching me how to get in shape using nothing but my bodyweight.

Success: Within a short period of time, I was not only able to start working out again, but I was able to get in the best shape of my life without ever walking back into a gym or injuring my back again.

Boom. Done. Within three sentences, you know my backstory and why I do what I do. At least, why I did what I did back then as a fitness coach.

Let me give you another example, this time from my current business. Okay, here is my new backstory for this business in three sentences:

Struggle: When I was 25 years old, I was broke and struggling to make ends meet.

Transition: Then, I read a book by Dan Kennedy that suggested writing a book to position myself as an authority in my field and have clients seeking me out instead of me seeking them out.

Success: Within twelve months of writing my book, I was able to generate more leads and referrals than ever before, dramatically increase my closing ratio, and even raise my prices.

Again, within three sentences, you know my backstory and why I do what I do. This may take you some time and effort to widdle the details down to only three sentences. But the time you spend on this exercise now will be worth its weight in gold when you're all done.

I used to think having a backstory was silly until I learned from my friend, James Malinchak, that people won't truly listen to you until they know you. In other words, the more someone knows about you, the more likely they are to listen to you, relate to you, and trust you. After all, we typically tell personal stories to friends. By telling people your backstory, you're befriending them and building a foundation of trust. And remember, all business starts with trust. If your audience doesn't trust you, then they won't buy from you.

Why Only 3 Sentences?

Now, you may be wondering why I had you write your backstory in only three sentences. The reason is simple. When you can tell your story in three, easy sentences, others can easily remember and tell your story in three, easy sentences.

That's the secondary purpose of your three-sentence story… to get told over and over and over again. When others can understand your story, they'll tell your story to others. This simple act of your story getting passed around not only helps you build trust faster, but the retelling helps you create an even stronger authority position now and into the future.

Okay, with that said, please understand that you can tell a longer version of your story if you have more time with your audience. For example, if I'm talking to someone at a networking event and we have just a little bit of time together, then I will tell him my three-sentence story. Doing so starts to build trust as well as intrigue. Most people will ask for more details, which allows the conversation to continue and go somewhere.

However, if I'm giving a presentation and I have more time, then I typically talk about my struggle all by itself for several minutes and go into more detail. The goal here is to paint the full picture. For example, in my current backstory, I talk about the pain I went through when I was broke and struggling. How I had a three-year old at the time. How my relationship was on the ropes because of our financial situation. How I was working both day and night to make my dreams come true. And how all this made me feel like less of a man and a failure.

The bottom line is this: when you have more time, you can give more details. When you have less time, give less details. And no matter how much time you have, tell your story in a concise, interesting way that makes people listen and allows them to pass your message and your story onto someone else.

Okay, before you move on to the next chapter, jot down some additional details about your backstory. How did your main struggle cause other struggles in your life? How did that make you feel? How did that affect other areas of your life?

Then, do the same for your transition and your success. What other details may be pertinent or interesting. How did your newfound success make you feel? How did it change the direction of your life? Do this now before moving on so you have these details ready to go when you tell your story to others.

13

Your Character's Qualities & Tendencies

As a reminder, there are three components to creating your unique Authority Character:

1. Your character's backstory
2. Your character's qualities and tendencies
3. Your character's philosophy

With your new and improved backstory to grab attention, keep people interested, and start building trust, let's look at the qualities and tendencies you'll want to focus on and the new traits you'll want to incorporate.

I want to remind you that you don't have to settle on ONE Authority Type. You can blend specific qualities together to create your own unique Authority Character. Also, realize that we're not trying to change who you are. You have to be who you are. But that's not to say you can't become a better version of yourself. You're not creating the character you are; you're creating the character you want to be. The best version of yourself. As an authority, you're going to get more exposure than ever before. Show the world who you really are and who you've become or who you're becoming.

Okay, using the four types of authorities as a guide, which Authority Type do you best relate to and which character traits do you already possess. As a reminder:

1. **A Fighter** is an authority who is in the trenches fighting with you and showing you how he or she has done it. Fighters don't like to play games. They don't have time for B.S. or shenanigans. Fighters aren't afraid to get their hands dirty.

2. **A Mage** is an authority who can stand the heat of the spotlight if he or she needs to, but he prefers to stay back and help from a distance. Mages are not in an authority role to be seen as an authority. They are reluctant heroes. Mages are typically mild-mannered, subtle, and sophisticated.

3. **A Healer** is an authority who is on a mission to search out and bring you the best possible information and solutions he or she can find. Healers can be very opinionated and can be seen as crusaders who will stop at nothing to support you on your journey.

4. **A Rogue** is an authority who "takes" other authorities' information and presents it to you in his own,

unique way. They are reporters at heart and seek the truth about their area of expertise. Rogues are natural learners, and they read and research a lot of books. Rogues tend to keep to themselves and remain in the shadows.

Like I said before, I personally relate best to the Mage and the Fighter. I tend to play a reluctant hero because I genuinely feel obligated to show you how to do what I've done, so you can reach your own personal goals and dreams. I also don't mind standing in the background and not being the center of attention when it comes to your success. At the same time, I also like to play the role of a Fighter because this role comes naturally to me, and being in charge is part of who I am.

I also want to point out that I have other qualities from the other characters. For instance, I'm passionate to the point of fanatical about my work, like the Healer. And I love reading, learning, and bringing my clients great information, like the Rogue. Remember, we all have qualities from all four types. We just tend to relate better to one or two of the types.

So, now it's your turn. Which authority type or types do you best relate to? In addition, what are some other traits you possess from the other characters. Take a moment and jot these traits down.

Making Your Character Real

Now that you have some of the traits written down, let's quickly look at how to make your character more real. How?

By looking at our imperfections and owning them. You see, every human being is flawed in some way. No one is perfect. And the authority you're about to become cannot be perfect either. All people, including your ideal, target audience, can't relate to someone who's perfect. Actually, people resent people they perceive as perfect. And remember, perception is reality, so we don't want to appear perfect.

Instead, we want people to see our best qualities shining through, while giving them a glimpse at our imperfections. I call the good traits **Heroic Qualities** – qualities you want people to see immediately. And I call the imperfect traits **Dark-Side Tendencies** – tendencies you want people to see, but you understand that these negative traits may turn some prospects off.

For example, a Fighters' attitude may give off a vibe that says, "of course it's going to be hard, but here's how to do it." That's a Heroic Quality. In this case, the Fighter is being honest and telling you the truth you need to hear. Some people may try to sugar coat the facts. Not the Fighter. That's a great quality to have and show off.

On the flip side, a Fighters' attitude may also give off the vibe, "you're a loser if you don't do this and make this happen." That's a Dark-Side Tendency. In this instance, the Fighter is being honest but maybe a little too blunt. That directness can turn some people off. It all depends on who you're targeting. If you're targeting someone who enjoys directness, then this trait will help you build trust with him faster. However, if you're ideal audience doesn't like direct-

> We want people to see our best qualities shining through, while giving them a glimpse at our imperfections.

ness but can take the occasional dose of candor, understand that this tendency should be shown to your audience in small amounts.

Other Heroic Qualities you may possess or you may want to possess could be: "I'm nothing special. If I can do it anyone can do it." Or, "I don't have all the answers, but I'm on a mission to serve you." You may want to consider adopting both of these Heroic Qualities. After all, the more heroic you look, the more authority and power you demonstrate.

Other Dark-Side Tendencies you may possess or see in yourself could be: over selling your ideas, flat out plagiarizing others' ideas and not making things your own, or being arrogant and condescending. These are tendencies you'll want to work on eliminating. As you become an authority, you're also becoming a better person in the process. Some imperfections are good for people to see and good for you to hold onto. Other Dark-Side Tendencies should be eradicated.

Take a moment now before moving on to the next chapter and jot down some Heroic Qualities you'd like to show off or adopt, as well as some Dark-Side Tendencies you'd like to eliminate or tone down.

And remember, you're not trying to change who you are. You're strategically creating a better version of yourself. You're creating the new, unique Authority Character you want to be. The Authority Character you want your target audience to see, trust, and do business with.

14

Your Character's Philosophy

Okay, so you've flushed out your new, Authority Character's backstory, as well as the Heroic Qualities you want to show off and the Dark-Side Tendencies you want to eliminate or tone down. Let's look at the final piece to this critical and profitable puzzle: your character's philosophy.

Your character's philosophy is based around what you value and what you stand for. For example, Tony Robbins is all about helping you create massive change in your life by conditioning yourself for success. That's his philosophy. In addition, he values personal responsibility and power, providing more value than anyone expects, and focusing on the relationships in your life. I don't know about you, but I resonate with his philosophy, and I relate to his values. That's probably why I've bought almost every course and book he's come out with and why I've been listening to him for over 25 years.

My resonance with his material is not just about the content he produces. It's about what he believes in and stands for. Since I resonate with his philosophy, I continue to read, watch, and listen to what he has to say. In my mind, he's an authority on the subject of personal development and personal performance.

Does that mean I don't listen to other authorities on this topic? Not at all. But I've invested more time and money with Tony than any other authority in this field because of his philosophy.

Let me give you another example. A new authority I recently started watching and listening to is Dave Ramsey. If you don't know of Dave Ramsey, his area of expertise is helping people get out of debt using Christian-based rules for money, and he values faith, common sense, and following a proven system.

Now, while I don't value his faith and belief system (I respect his belief system but don't believe what he believes), I value and resonate with what he says and what he stands for. In fact, he's summed up his philosophy in one sentence and I believe in the sentiment whole-heartily: "Live like no one else, so later you can live and give like no one else." I've never seen a philosophy summed up like that. It's simple, concise, and powerful.

Now, what about you? What do you stand for? What do you value most? In just a moment, we're going to look at this idea in more depth. But first, realizing that your values and your philosophy should match up with your ideal audience's values is important to keep in mind.

Do you remember the exercises we did in Chapters 7 and 8, where you wrote down the values and motives your ideal audience shares? You can use that information as a jumping off point if you'd like. Take the ideas you already have written down and use those as your foundation to build your own philosophy. If you haven't already, you'll soon discover that your best clients will share your value system and your core philosophy.

What Are You Against?

Okay, there is one more thing I want you to consider. And this is just as important as knowing what you value and what you stand for. What are you against?

Have you ever rooted for the underdog in a movie or in real life? Of course, you have. We all have at one point or another. Why? Why do we root for the underdog? Yes, we sometimes root for the underdogs because we share the same values they do, or we resonate with their beliefs and philosophy. But, more often than not, we root for the underdog because he has been wronged in some way. When someone is being mistreated, wronged, or abused by another person or by an establishment, and that victimization goes against our personal values and beliefs, we stand up and fight. We fight for the underdog. We fight against what we believe is wrong. And we fight against the offender and the offensive act.

That's why having a philosophy that not only resonates with your audience's values is important, but having a philosophy that opposes someone or something else is extremely powerful. When we oppose someone or something else that we know is wrong, we'll win the attention, respect, and connection of others who feel and believe as we feel and believe.

So, as this idea relates to your business and industry, what are you against? Is there a concept or group of people you're firmly against? Personally, for my own business, one concept I'm against is writing a book to make money with book sales. I tell my fans, followers, and clients all the time: the real money in publishing a book is positioning yourself as an authority and leading clients to your backend profit centers. Can you make money from book sales? Yes. But that's not where the real money is. Making money solely from book sales is a concept I'm against. And using a book as a tool is a concept that rings true with my best clients.

Think about other authorities you may know today. One of my favorite authors is Dan Kennedy, who has written a series of books based on his No B.S. philosophy. A few book titles

> "People will follow you if you stand for their beliefs or fight against their opposition."
> ~Weston Lyon

are: *No B.S. Sales Success, No B.S. Time Management for Entrepreneurs,* and *No B.S. Ruthless Management of People & Profits*. Dan's No B.S. philosophy is about going against the norm and doing what other successful business renegades have done to grow their businesses. He's against branding experts who can't show you a return on your advertising efforts. And he's against the woo-hoo, sit in the lotus position and meditate until you become successful philosophy. By being against these concepts and people, he attracts a loyal following who believe in his philosophy and are against the same concepts and people he is.

I heard Dave Ramsey say on a recent YouTube video (I'm summarizing here), "A lot of people don't like me (insurance agents, bankers, car dealers) because I tell it the way it is, and I help you see through their scams and ploys. But 8 million of you do like what I'm saying. That's who I care about and who I help. You!"

That was a brilliant way of demonstrating his authority and letting his audience, new listeners and seasoned fans, know that he is against the scams and ploys insurance agents, bankers, and car dealers try to pull. I'm a new listener, so I can tell you that his message not only resonated with me, but this message strengthened the faith I have in his opinions and instructions.

You want to do the same with your audience. You want to be against something or someone that your audience is against, so you demonstrate *your* authority and strengthen *your* message so you cultivate a stronger bond with them.

So, in your business and industry, what are you against? Take some time right now before moving on and jot down some of the values, philosophies, concepts, and people you're against.

BE AUTHORITY-PRESENT

This is where the rubber meets the road, and where you start putting all these parts together to become the authority you are meant to be and serve the people you are meant to serve!

As a quick recap, you first learned that you don't have to be an authority *yet* to be perceived as an authority. With the right intention, you can ethically position yourself as an authority and start helping your ideal, target audience right now. Then, you learned what real authorities do, how they behave, and what people expect from real authorities. Remember, perception is reality. So, to be perceived as an expert, you have to do what real authorities do and behave how real authorities behave. If you don't, then people won't *see* you as an expert – even if you *are* a real authority. That's the trap. To be seen as a real authority, you must *demonstrate* your authority. And you can do just that with my five-step formula...

Step 1: Be Relevant

Step One is all about *what* you say. You now know that you have to be relevant. And to be relevant, you have to know, understand, empathize with, and talk to your ideal, target audience about the situation they're currently experiencing: what fears they are trying to avoid; what desires they are trying to achieve; what drivers they value most; and what motives they rely on to move them forward and help them transition from their current situation to a new, ideal situation.

Step 2: Be Interesting

Step Two is all about *how* you say what you say. Yes, you must be relevant to grab your audience's attention, but you now know that making your message interesting and unique is just as important. And the easiest way to make your message interesting is by making yourself interesting, unique, and creating a better version of yourself to show the world.

We call that new, better version of yourself your unique, Authority Character. And we talked about how you can best relate to your ideal audience by telling them your backstory: how you or someone you know struggled, transitioned by finding a better way, and ultimately succeeded in some way, shape, or form.

We then augmented your Authority Character by showing your audience your Heroic Qualities and Dark-Side Tendencies so they see that you're a real person and not some perfect, fake authority.

Lastly, we endeared your audience to you by conveying your living, breathing philosophy: who you are, what you stand for, and what you are aggressively against.

So, that's where we are. The remainder of this book will focus on the final three steps and how you can demonstrate and leverage your new, authority position. Those final, three steps are:

Step 3: Be Authority-Present

Step 4: Be Talkable

Step 5: Be Undeniable

Be Authority-Present

Step Three is all about *where* you say what you say. Being Authority-Present is about being everywhere other authorities are. Listen, in our society, certain types of people command authority. According to author and professional copywriter, Dan S. Kennedy, there are three types of professionals that command authority: Authors, Speakers, and Celebrities/Media Personalities.

You know of Steven King, J.K. Rowling, and Deepak Chopra because they write books. You know of the late, greats Zig

Ziglar, Jim Rohn, and Dr. Wayne Dyer because they spoke to audiences all over the world. You know of Oprah Winfrey, Ellen DeGeneres, and other celebrities because they've been on T.V. and in the media.

You know about these professionals not just because of what they've done or what they do, but because of how and where they spread their messages: in books, on stages, and in the media.

Do you think Bill O'Reilly could educate and persuade millions of Americans teaching history to high school? He tried. It didn't work. That's why he chose to go back to school for journalism and get into the media. The media is where his authority and power come from.

Do you think Zig Ziglar could have completely changed the sales industry just by going to a company's office and teaching sales training to their employees? Nope. Impossible. According to his sales and live appearances, Ziglar is estimated to have reached and influenced over 250 million people. That's a lot of people! Only his books and his speeches gave him that amazing opportunity to effect so many.

The list goes on and on, but I think you get the gist. How and where you spread your message will position you as a trusted authority and give you access to more opportunities, more people, and more money than you have right now.

So, how do you become an authority and stand out from the crowd? How do you become authority-present? Like we've previously discussed, you must do what other authorities do, behave how they behave, and (in this case) you must be where other authorities are: in books, on stage, and in the media.

It's time to buckle up and hold on to your seat. Over the next few chapters, we're going to talk about writing a book, becoming a speaker, and getting into the media.

15

Writing a Book

To become authority-present, you must write a book. There are no "ifs, ands, or buts" about it. Authorities are authors. And authors are authorities. Period. Now, I'm not going to show you how to write a book in this chapter. That's a bigger project that takes way more time than we have here. In fact, I have a course on how to write a book called the *Book Publishing Protocol*, and the writing section alone consists of a 120-page manual and 14 videos. That task would be very overwhelming at this point since we're only halfway through this book, so we're not going to tackle writing a book today. Instead, what I'd like to do is get you started down that path and have you start thinking about writing a book.

What's Your Book About?

What can your book be about? I know, the possibilities seem endless, right? And to some extent the possibilities are indeed endless. But when you're thinking about writing your

> **BONUS!**
>
> If you're interested in writing a book (and you should be), at the end of this book on pages 241-242, you'll find details on how you can gain access to my *Fast Start to Book Writing Success* course (*a $97 value*) absolutely free.

book, your book should be about taking your audience from where they are now to where they want to be.

That should sound familiar. Remember… to be relevant to your ideal audience you have to talk to them about the situation they're currently experiencing. These situations are what they're hyper-aware of right now, and that's what they really want to learn about. They want to learn how to get out of or away from their current circumstance and find greener pastures.

At your book's core, these struggles and circumstances are what you should write about. So, let me ask you a question: how can you take your ideal audience from where they are, from the situation they're currently in, to where they want to be?

Is there a process you could show them? Are there some tips or tricks you could teach them? That's what you want to write about – that's your book. And ironically, this process or tricks are also the speech you want to give and the ideas you want to share with the media.

Look, being an expert isn't about constantly creating new and better information for your audience. Yes, that's part of being an authority, but you'll do that over years and decades. You don't have to start out with a library full of ideas. You just have to start off with one idea that will take your audience from where they are to where they want to be.

Think about the books you've read over your lifetime. Why did you choose them? Like most people, you probably chose the majority of books you've read because they promised to solve a problem or help you achieve a desired end result.

I hope this sounds familiar. The same stuff we covered earlier in this book can now be used in your book, in your speech, and with the media. Your audience wants to conquer their fears. They want to achieve their desires. And they want to live life with what they value most. These fears, desires, and values are what your book should be about.

Capture Your Ideas

The first step to writing your book is to capture as many ideas about your topic as you can. Here's a short list of questions to ask yourself to help you come up with ideas for your book:

1. What questions are you asked the most about your topic?
2. What questions are you asked the least - but should be asked because they're important to know?

3. What are some common misconceptions about your topic?

4. What are some secrets and/or tricks-of-the-trade about your industry?

5. What are some common trouble areas or pitfalls-to-avoid in your industry?

6. How do your prospects use what you sell?

7. How do your prospects do what you do?

8. What are three to five steps someone can take to get results?

These questions will get your mind racing and allow you to come up with a long list of ideas to write about. Remember, the point is to capture as many ideas as you can.

Now, to do this quickly and easily, don't write down your ideas in sentence format (unless you think better that way). Instead, try jotting down your ideas in a two to five-word phrases with just enough context to jog your memory when you move into the writing step. Taking notes this way will allow you to get more ideas written down faster without losing any ideas and keeping your momentum moving full steam ahead.

How many ideas should you come up with? I recommend shooting for a combined list of 50-100 tips, questions, mistakes, stories, etc. That way, you have enough content to choose from when you move into the next step of writing your book.

> "Authorities are authors. And authors are authorities."

Last, don't edit your thoughts and ideas. There are no stupid ideas because ideas come from ideas. Filtering your ideas now only clips your wings and limits your true potential. At the same time, do not to get lost in the thinking process and don't get caught up in all the details surrounding your ideas. Simply capture your ideas. Period. You'll have time to prune, edit, expand upon, and delete ideas later. For now, let your mind overflow with ideas about your topic and theme.

To give you an example of how I do this when I write a book, here are the initial ideas I captured when I started writing my last book, *The Most Powerful Business Tool Ever to Exist*.

- Fears of writing a book
- Power of writing
- Positioning as an authority
- Positioning with the media
- Marketing strategies with a book
- Leveraging a book
- Bill Phillips and EAS
- Unique Message
- Honing your message
- Packaging

- Back-end sales
- Print Ads
- Online Ads
- Meeting new people and authorities
- Direct Mail
- Networking & Prospecting
- Referrals
- Customer lifecycle
- Joint Ventures
- Information products
- Books as business cards
- Speaking
- Book as bonus
- Keep appointments
- Customer reactivating
- Unique product
- Increase confidence
- Giving back
- Paul Zane Pilzer story

There are 29 total ideas here that turned into a 182-page book. Again, I recommend you shooting for a combined list of 50-100 tips, questions, mistakes, stories, etc. to make your job easier. I know… there's only 29 ideas above. But you must remember that I've written eighteen books prior to this book. I know a thing or two about how my writing process works and how my mind works. Since this is most likely your first time writing a book, I highly suggest getting 50-100 ideas down on paper.

I feel that you'll find this exercise invaluable. Also, please note that you can use this exercise in conjunction with my **Fast Start to Book Writing Success** course that I'm gifting you at the end of this book. But I'm getting a little ahead of myself. We'll focus on writing your first book (or your next book) after you've finished reading this book. Okay, in the next chapter, we'll explore another way for you to become authority-present: speaking on stage.

16

Speaking on Stage

Let's continue our discussion on becoming authority-present. First, we know that authorities write books. But that's not all authorities do. Authorities are also speakers. Over the next two chapters, we're going to explore the ins and outs of becoming a speaker as well as the six steps to giving an unforgettable speech.

But before we get into this topic, I have to bring up the elephant in the room. Most people are scared to death of speaking. Actually, I've seen studies that show that most people fear speaking on stage more than they fear death. I find that a little far-fetched, but whether it's 100% accurate or not isn't the point. The point is, most people are scared to get up on stage and talk to an audience.

That's a real fear that unfortunately paralyses a lot of people. And while I'm not a psychiatrist or expert on getting over that fear, I can tell you from personal experience that I had that fear when I first began speaking on stage. I know what it feels like to have your heart beating out of your chest. I know what it feels like to have sweat dripping down the sides of your body and trickling down your arms and off your wrists. I know what that feels like. And it's not a good feeling. However, I can also tell you that the fear of speaking from the stage is like any other fear. It's in your head, and you can take control and eliminate the fear if you have enough reasons why.

So, what was my reason for conquering that particular fear? I know this is going to sound overly simplistic, but I wanted to be seen as an authority, and I knew that authorities were authors and speakers. So, I got up and started speaking from stage. Was speaking easy at first? No way. It was hard, and it was scary. But after getting up a few times, speaking became easier and easier. And like anything you do multiple times and see results from, getting up in front of an audience eventually started to become fun.

Today, speaking is one of my absolute favorite things to do. I love the thrill of getting on stage or on a webinar and showing people how to do something – be it write a book, position themselves as authorities, or whatever. I've done hundreds and hundreds of talks, and I've spoken to thousands and thousands of people.

Now, this isn't about me as a speaker. It's about you. I just wanted to share that fear with you because I know a lot of people are afraid of speaking. And in case you missed my point, if you suffer from the fear of speaking, one of the keys to getting over this fear is to come up with reasons why you want to speak.

Yes, speaking will still be scary at first, but if you're armed with a handful of solid reasons for getting up on stage, you'll have the guts to get up and start. And once you start, you'll gain a little confidence. And then a little more. And a little more. Until speaking becomes second nature for you and dare I say fun. If you suffer from the fear of speaking, give that exercise a little try and let me know how it works for you.

The Two Types of Stages

There are two types of stages you can speak from:

1. Someone Else's Stage
2. Your Own Stage

By far, when most people think of speaking, they think of speaking from someone else's stage. So, whether you're traveling all over the world, speaking at corporations, colleges, business seminars, and trade associations or simply getting up and speaking at your local chamber, networking events, and rotary meetings, you're speaking on someone else's stage. In other words, someone else has set up the meeting or event. Someone else has organized the agenda. Someone else has spent money marketing the event. And someone else has enticed attendees to show up to see you and maybe some other speakers.

With that said, speaking from someone else's stage isn't the only option. You can also create your own stage and speak from it. In the old days, this process would take a lot more planning and money because you'd have to do the event live and in-person at a hotel or some other venue. And while that's a great option, in today's digital world, this isn't the only way to organize your own talk or build your own stage. You can now hold live events like webinars, online seminars, and Facebook live events, etc. from the comfort of your own home or create and host your own YouTube channel. Yes, these options will still take some planning and expense, but not nearly the same as holding a live event.

Personally, I've done both types of speaking. I've spoken for small, local groups as well as large national associations. In addition, I've also held my own events, both live/ in-person and on the internet. They both have their pros and cons. I started speaking on someone else's stage before creating my own. However, if I were to start all over, I'd consider starting with your own online events that you can invite people to as you get more comfortable with your material and talking to more people. Then, I'd venture out to speaking on someone else's stage, first at small, local events, then at bigger and bigger meetings and seminars. Finally, I'd start hosting bigger online events and live, in-person events.

But look, I'm not here to tell you which type of speaking will be best for you or which venues to choose. Those are just my suggestions after speaking to audiences of all shapes and sizes for almost two decades now. These decisions are yours. I just want you to realize that you can do either – speak on someone else's stage or speak on your own stage – to position yourself as an authority. And whatever you decide to do, know that speaking in general can be very rewarding and very profitable.

The Two Types of Speeches

Okay, once you decide which type of stage to speak on, let's look at what type of speech you can give. There are two types of speeches:

1. Fee-Based Speeches
2. Free Speeches

Fee-based speeches are pretty straight-forward. A meeting planner or an event promoter contracts you to speak for a specific fee. You give the speech, and they pay you. Like any business deal, everything is up for negotiation, but you typically get half the money up front to hold the date and half after the service is rendered (i.e. you speak for their audience).

Your fee is up to you too. You can charge $500, $1500, $5,000, etc. Whatever you want and whatever you can negotiate is fair game. Of course, what you can negotiate usually depends on the type of client you're going after. For instance, one of my clients speaks to local companies for a couple thousand dollars a speech. Another client speaks to high schools for a few hundred dollars a speech. And on the other end of the spectrum, a friend of mine speaks at large corpora-

> Yes, you can speak for free and still get paid... if you know how.

tions for $12,000 a speech. As you can see, the fees range based on target audience. I'm not saying that's the only factor you should look at when choosing a target audience, but that's a big factor.

Two other important factors are the speaker's skill level and the speaker's confidence to ask for more money. And out of all three factors, skill level is the least important. In my opinion, the audience matters most because if they don't have the money to pay for your talk or expertise, you can ask for your fee but never stand a chance of receiving your full fee. And the second most important factor is your level of confidence to ask for what you're worth.

The second type of speech, the free speech, is more common but less understood. There are two ways to give a free speech and still get results worth your time and effort. First, there's the…

Content-Only Speech

The content-only speech is where an event promoter contracts you to speak to his group or organization for free in exchange for "exposure" to his audience. I used to think these types of speeches were only for newbies learning the ropes of the speaking industry. After all, I once heard that you can die from exposure. Honestly, I laugh when people talk about exposure. I'm not interested in exposure. I'm interested in results. And you can prosper from a free speech if you know what to do. In fact, my friend, Sue Henry, actually teaches how she makes tens of thousands of dollars from free speeches. I'm not going to teach you her entire system, but I will share the two vital components you need to profit from a free speech.

First, you need a way to capture the audience's contact information. You can have them turn in their business cards, fill out a form, text you on their phone, etc. Why would they do this? Because in addition to the free information you're providing them, you're also going to give them something else for free. That something else could be your book, a video course, a resource guide, or anything else that's valuable and they desperately want from you.

Then, once you have their contact info (name and email at the very least), you can follow-up with them. This follow-up is the key to any good lead-generation system. You must learn to be good at follow-up if you plan on being in business for any length of time. And the business of speaking, whether you speak as one of your lead generation tactics or you turn speaking into a full-blown business, is no exception. You must capture people's contact information and follow-up with them.

Not everyone is going to buy from you, but that's natural. Only a small percent will buy, but that's the percent that can make you wealthy… or at least well-compensated for your time.

Platform Selling

The second way to give a free speech is to sell from the platform. This is called "platform selling," and this type of speech is where an event promoter contracts you to speak to his group or organization for free in exchange for letting you sell products and/or services to his audience. You can sell your book or books. You can sell your more in-depth course. You can even sell your services. The skies the limit, and you're only restricted by your imagination.

Now, if you've never sold from the platform, I will tell you that platform selling is unlike anything you've done before. Platform selling is selling one-to-many, not one-to-one. So, selling this way is a completely different animal all together and will take lots of practice on your end to develop the skill. But, once you get the skill down, platform selling can be extremely powerful and profitable. In fact, the best platform sellers in the world prefer platform selling over fee-based selling. Why? Because the income potential is so much higher. For example, the best platform sellers can walk away from a speech with 20, 50, even $100,000 in their pockets – and that's after paying the promoter 50%. You read that correctly. The best platform sellers can make more in one or two speeches than the average American can make all year.

Like the types of stages you can speak from, the type of speech you give is up to you. However, I'd recommend starting off with free speeches where you give something away in exchange for your audience's contact information. Then, once you feel comfortable speaking to larger and larger audiences,

I'd recommend moving into fee-based speaking. Finally, once you have plenty of experience making offers from the stage, I'd recommend you start to sell from the platform.

That's not to say you can't do all these from the get-go. You can. That's just the progression I'd recommend for most people. But please don't let me hold you back. If you feel confident charging a fee from the start or selling from the stage from day one, go for it. Only you can decide if you're ready. Just don't get frustrated if something doesn't work out. That's life. Things are going to go awry. Things are going to fall flat or blow up in your face. That's just par for the course. Understand that, be mentally prepare for that, and you'll be good to go.

One final point about free speeches is this: don't forget that you can speak on your own stage too. So, for example, you can set up your own online seminar and invite your current clients, networking buddies, prospects, etc. and give them 100% content or sell them something. You don't have to find an event promoter. You can do this all yourself if you'd like. And again, you can get results from either type of speech: content only or platform selling.

17

6 Steps to Giving an Unforgettable Speech

Okay, so no matter which type of stage or which type of speech you give, the next question you're probably asking yourself is, "How do I give a great speech?" I'm glad you asked because giving a great speech is at the heart to positioning yourself as an authority. After all, you can't give a lousy performance and expect people to think you're great or know what you're talking about. To position yourself as an authority, you have to be good.

Now, that's not to say you're going to be amazing the first time you get on stage. You probably won't be amazing. But you'll get better and better. In fact, that's why I suggested to you earlier that starting with your own online seminars or webinars may be the best place to start. Again, doing so will give you the necessary practice you need to get good. Actually, you don't even need anyone on the webinar with you. Just the act of speaking will make you better.

There's another thing I want you to know about being good. Being good is subjective. So, you don't have to wow the crowd, you just have to give good, solid advice and present your information in a clear, easy-to-follow format. That's the key to giving a good speech. So, if you're not dynamic and you're worried about not being charismatic, don't be. You don't have to be dynamic. If you don't know everything there is to know about your topic and you're worried about not being a walking encyclopedia, don't be. You don't have to know everything.

Again, the key to giving a good speech is to give good, solid advice and present your information in a clear, easy-to-follow format. With that said, let's look at the six steps to giving an unforgettable speech:

Step 1: Set the Stage

Before you even get on stage, start positioning yourself as an authority to the audience. You can do this in one of two ways. First, you can have a discussion with the person reading your introduction and coach him or her on what to say and how to say your intro. The goal here is to make sure whoever is introducing you is not winging it or ad-libbing. Give these people your introduction beforehand, and make sure they understand the importance of reading it or memorizing it verbatim. Why?

Because your introduction should include words and phrases that get your audience's attention. Remember earlier in this book when we talked about being relevant to your audience? Being relevant is what you have to do from the very start. Before you ever speak a word, the audience must be prepped by the promoter introducing you to let them know this presentation is worth listening to.

The second way you can start positioning yourself as an authority from the word "go" is to "introduce" yourself. No, I don't mean you want to literally introduce yourself from stage or behind the scenes. Instead, you can get your message across and not allow anyone to mess this up for you by creating a video to play before you go on stage. This type of video is called a "sizzle reel." It gets the crowd pumped up and has the same purpose as the person introducing you: to position you as the authority and prep the audience so they know you're worth listening to. Whichever method you choose, set the stage and you'll set yourself up for an unforgettable speech.

Step 2: Start with a Bang

After you're introduced by someone or by your sizzle reel, you want to start the speech off with a bang. You can do this in one of two ways. First, you can do something unexpected, unique, or profound. For example, one speaker I know starts his speech from the back of the room. Yep, while most speakers start from the front of the room on stage, he starts from the back of the room in the middle of the crowd. This simple change is completely unexpected and makes people pay attention from the start.

Another speaker I've seen repels from the rafters onto the stage. Yeah, repels. As in repels like a rock climber would from a rock face. The only difference is he repels from the rafters. As you can imagine, this entrance is nothing short of amazing. People are riveted and on the edge of their seats from the get go. Now, you don't have to do anything this extravagant or dangerous, but I think you get the point. When you do something unexpected to start your speech, you grab the audience's attention and change their state of mind from bored to riveted.

Now, a quick word of warning. Don't rely on this gimmickry to keep the audience's attention. The words you say after you do something like this are just as important for keeping them interested and letting them know you're worth their time.

This point leads me to the second way you can start your speech off with a bang. You can tell them something unique and/or unexpected. For example, one speaker I know starts his speeches off with a joke. Admittedly, this is a dangerous tactic because if the joke falls flat, the speech can die on the vine. However, he's a funny guy and most times pulls this tactic off without a hitch. So, if you can make a joke or anecdote work, this may be an option for you.

A better option though, and an option I see from plenty of speakers use, is to start your speech off with a powerful story. This is a great way to start your speech off with a bang. Find a powerful story to use or, preferably, craft your own unique powerful story with a moral that relates to your speech and you're golden. People love stories, and they're

> Start off with a bang by doing something unexpected, unique, or profound.

trained to listen to stories. Stories are your best friend when it comes to grabbing attention and getting a message across.

One more way to start your speech off with bang, and a way I recommend for both novices and advanced speakers, is to make a big promise. Platform speakers are famous for starting their speeches off this way, and it's an adaptation of the old, speaking adage: first, tell them what you're going to talk about. For instance, one platform speaker I've seen started his speech off by saying something like, "In the next 90 minutes, I'm going to show you how to double your business with three strategies you've never seen before."

That's a big promise, and it's a promise that pulls the listener into your speech because they:

a) want to double their business,

b) want to learn the three strategies, and

c) are intrigued and curious about what they don't know.

You can take this opener and tweak it for almost any speech. For example, if you're a fitness coach, you can start off with something like, "In the next 90 minutes, I'm going to show you how to lose twenty pounds in the next five weeks and keep the weight off forever with three strategies you've never seen before."

If you're a financial advisor for divorced housewives, you can start off with something like, "I know what you're going through. I've been there. So, in the next 90 minutes, I'm going to show you how to get back on your feet and financially thrive with three strategies you've never seen before."

Of course, you'll have to deliver on the goods. But if you can, then starting off with a promise like this is a smart way to kick off your speech with a bang, grab the audience's attention, and keep them engaged.

Step 3: Tell Your Story

Do you remember in Chapter 12 when I had you write down the details of your story in three sentences? This is the part of the speech where you tell them about your struggle, your transition, and your success. The point of telling your story here is to get your audience to relate to you and to like you. Throughout the speech that rapport will develop into trust because you're being honest and real with them.

The only tricky part is your transition into your story and out of your story. But have no fear. I'm going to give you an easy transition to use for each. First, the transition into your story. Let's use the "double your business" example. In this example, you start off with the big promise: in the next 90 minutes, I'm going to show you how to double your business with three strategies you've never seen before. You can then transition into your story by saying, "I know that may sound far-fetched, but let me tell you what happened to me."

That's it. The words "let me tell you what happened to me" easily transitions you into your story and allows you to talk about your struggle. So, if I were to use this opener, transition, and story with my business, it would sound something like this:

"In the next 90 minutes, I'm going to show you how to double your business with three strategies you've never seen before. I know that may sound far-fetched or maybe even a little bit hype-y, but let me tell you what happened to me. When I was 25 years old, I was broke and struggling to make ends meet. I had a 3-year old at the time and my relationship was on the ropes…"

See. An effortless transition from my opener to my story. What about the fitness coach example? You could say something like, "In the next 90 minutes, I'm going to show you how to lose twenty pounds in the next five weeks and keep the weight off forever with three strategies you've never seen before. I know that may sound crazy to you right now, but let me tell you what happened to me. When I was 47 years old, I was laid off from work and I quickly gained 28 pounds from a lot of emotional eating. My marriage was solid, but my mindset was way off…" Simple, right?

Step 4: Present 3-5 Main Ideas

This is going to be the bulk of your speech and where you demonstrate your authority by giving good, solid information that actually helps your audience members. Don't be afraid to give them some of your best stuff here. Remember, you have one chance to impress them with your knowledge and expertise. Don't hold back. Look, most entrepreneurs who become speakers to demonstrate authority and grow their businesses fall short here because they are afraid to give too much good information because people won't need their help afterward. This couldn't be further from the truth. People are people. And most people simply don't act on all the advice they're given. Sometimes it's laziness. Sometimes it's forgetfulness. But most of the time, you're going to find out that there are three types of people in your audience.

First, there are people who don't care enough to get the results you're talking about. You can't do anything with these people. They don't care enough to act on any information you give them, and they don't care enough to get your help and hire you.

Second, there are people who care so much about the results you're talking about that they'll fight other people in the room to talk with you afterwards. They want your information, and they want your help. No amount of free information will stop them from seeking you out. They need help, and they want you to help them.

The first and second type of person are on the extreme ends of the spectrum. The third type of person in your audience is somewhere in the middle. He or she wants your information but aren't sold on implementing your prescribed tactics yet. If you give these people piss poor information that they can't use, then they'll forget about you and buy from someone else who gives them what they need. However, if you give them great information, some of your best information, then they'll see you as the authority and want more of you. Giving them

> "Don't be afraid to give your audience some of your best stuff."

your best information doesn't matter. They'll want more because they rationalize that if this is the information you gave in only 60 or 90 minutes, then you must know a lot more.

So you see, giving your audience anything less than your best just doesn't make sense. The first group won't implement the information or buy from you anyway. The second group will buy from you no matter what. And the third group will only buy from you if they see the value you bring to the table. So again, anything less than your best will shoot you in the foot and depress your overall results as a speaker.

Okay, with that being said, what do you present here and why only three to five main points? First, you only present three to five main points because that's all you have time for. Anything more than five will water down your message. I prefer to stick to three main points because, for whatever reason, people can easily grasp three concepts. I can't remember where I heard this concept before, but one speaker I heard a long time ago said this: people count like this, "One, two, three, many." Meaning, when you start talking about more than three concepts, people get lost and uninterested. Of course, that's not true for everyone, but it's a good rule of thumb for audiences who don't know you yet.

As for what you present, you want to present concepts that will help your audience get the results they desire. If you're following my advice and starting off by giving them a big promise at the beginning of your speech – like "In the next 90 minutes, I'm going to show you how to lose twenty pounds in the next five weeks and keep the weight off forever with three strategies you've never seen before" or "In the next 90 minutes, I'm going to show you how to get back on your feet and financially thrive with three strategies you've never seen before" – then your three main points will be about those three strategies.

Simply tell them what the strategy is all about, how you found it or came up with it, the benefits of using the strategy, what the strategy has done for you, and a little bit about how the strategy works. Remember, this is a speech and not a hands-on workshop. You can't possibly teach them everything there is to know about the strategy in the time you have. But you can give them enough information to sink their teeth into as well as enough information to whet their appetite.

Okay, last point I want to make on the three to five main points of your speech. How do you transition into this part from your story? If we go back to the example on making the promise of doubling your business, you can transition into your main points by coming out of the success part of your story and saying something like, "That's how I went from broke and struggling to growing my business in just twelve months. Now, I want to show you exactly how I did it."

Boom…that's your transition: "Now I want to show you exactly how I did it."

I must point out that you don't want to make any false claims, nor do you want the audience to think they can do what you did and get the same results. I'm not a lawyer, but you can get into trouble if you make false claims or lead them to thinking they can succeed like you have. That's why it's ethical, less hype-y, and easier to tell them that you're going to show them how you succeeded, and let them know that there are too many factors to guarantee their success. You can only tell them what you did and allow them to make their own decisions.

One more quick side note about putting this disclaimer into your speech. At first, you may think this type of disclaimer would hinder your authority. It actually does the opposite and positions you with even more power. Why? In my personal opinion, giving a disclaimer like this subconsciously tells the audience that you're not pulling the wool over their eyes. You're being honest and ethical. And you're treating them like friends instead of fools who can be misled. Of course, that's exactly what you want to do anyway. You don't want to swindle anyone. You want to give them the best advice you can and help them succeed with your advice. So, this type of disclaimer is not only necessary but very beneficial.

Step 5: Future Pace

What is "future pacing" and how do you do it? First, future pacing is when you help the audience visualize their future, and you show them what life would be like if they simply follow your plan. Again, we're not guaranteeing them this future, but we are letting them get a glimpse of what's possible. For example, in the doubling your business example, you say something like, "In five years, what would your business look like if you successfully used these three strategies? Imagine having more clients. Imagine having more income and profits. What about your lifestyle? Imagine working less. Imagine taking more vacation time. Imagine playing more with your kids. Imagine taking your spouse on weekend getaways. And imagine having more time for yourself. Can you imagine these things happening?"

That's future pacing. You're allowing the audience to dream a little bit, so they can see that the strategies or tips you just gave them mean more than just growing their business. There are more powerful benefits to this growth. And they need to see those benefits before you sell them anything. Again, we're not trying to give them false hope or trick them in any way. We're simply showing them what's possible. And we're reminding them of what they really want anyway.

Most entrepreneurs don't get into business just to be in business. We all have other motives, right? We want something from our business. That "something" may be more money to get out of debt and have more things. It may be to have more free time for ourselves and our family. The list goes on and on, and that's what we want our audience to think about. We want to show them what their future could look like if they use our strategies.

This step is relatively short. Maybe a few minutes if all you're doing is future pacing like I showed you. Maybe a little longer if you throw in a story about your clients and what they're futures turned into. Again, if you have time, tell stories whenever you can. People are programmed to listen to stories, and stories help you get your point across without any resistance.

Okay, how do you transition into this step? You can simple say something like, "So there you have it. Those are the same three strategies I've used in my business to double my sales in the past twelve months. Let me ask you this: five years from now, what would your business look like if you successfully used these exact same strategies?" Then, simply future pace by telling them to imagine benefit one, benefit two, benefit three, and so on. "Imagine having more clients. Imagine having more income and profits. Imagine working less. Imagine taking more vacation time. Etc."

If we use the fitness coach example, it would sound something like, "So there you have it. Those are the same three strategies I've used to help clients just like you lose twenty pounds in only five weeks and keep the weight off for years and decades to come. Let me ask you this: five years from now, what would you look like and how would you feel if you successfully used these exact same strategies? Imagine being twenty pounds lighter. Imagine feeling ten years younger. Imagine life with a new body and a new spirit. Imagine having more energy and more quality years in your life."

Step 6: Present the Solution

Now that you've set yourself up for success with your introduction, grabbed your audience's attention with your big promise, built a rapport and started to establish trust with your story, kept their attention and interest with your best information, and allowed them to see what their perfect future could look like, let's move them to action by offering your solution.

This is where most speakers drop the ball completely. Why? Because they change their tone and begin to sell the audience on their solution. While this is exactly what you're doing – selling – keep your tone the same and offer the audience members a solution to their problems. I'll repeat that. You're not hard-selling them. You're offering them a solution. So, let's first talk about the transition into this final step.

If we look at the doubling your business example one last time, the transition would sound something like this: "I hope you've enjoyed learning this information as much as I've enjoyed showing it to you. If you're interested in my step-by-step plan to double your business in the next twelve months, then let me show you how I can help you."

That's it. Simply offer to help them by showing them how you can help. After you transition into the final step, make your offer simply a matter of showing them what you have. Give them all the details they need to make an educated decision while throwing in more useful content and stories to illustrate the benefits to what you're offering. Don't make this step overly complicated. Just tell people what you've got, how much your services or packages cost, and what results they should expect.

> "You must tell your audience exactly what to do and not leave anything up to chance."

In regard to cost, remember that you can sell the audience a book, some other product, a service, or give them something for free in exchange for their contact information. In all three cases, the final step is the same. You're telling them what you've got, how much it costs (if anything), and what results they should expect.

Last, tell them how they can take advantage of this opportunity. If the offer is free, are they filling out a form you've passed to them, are they texting you, are they emailing you, or are they going to your website? You get the gist. If you're selling them a product or service, do they have to come to the back of the room? Whatever the action is, you must tell them exactly what to do and not leave anything up to chance. Trust me when I tell you this, you cannot be too thorough when it comes to getting them to take the proper action. Redundancy is your best friend in this step of the process.

Okay, so I've shown you everything you need to know to become a speaker and give a great speech. Remember, becoming a speaker is a sure-fire way to become and remain authority-present. In the next chapter, we'll look at getting into the media to position yourself as an authority and celebrity in your niche as well as ways to ethically manufacture your authority and celebrity.

18

Getting Into the Media

Let's look at getting into the media, expanding your reach, and positioning yourself as an authority and celebrity in your field. How are we going to do this? Well, like the two types of stages you can speak from, there are two types of media platforms you can enter:

1. Someone Else's Media Platform
2. Your Own Media Platform

Someone Else's Media Platform

This type of platform is more well-known because it's seen every day. "Someone else's media platform" includes TV, radio, and print media. So for example, when you see an author or some other authority on a local TV station giving the viewers tips, that authority is on someone else's media platform. In this case, the TV station's platform. If you hear an authority being interviewed on the radio, they're on someone else's media platform (i.e. the radio station's platform). And when you read a quote from an authority or see a print interview with an authority, they're using the print media's platform. You can enter someone else's media platform by approaching these media outlets and pitching your ideas to them.

Pitching your idea is typically done by using a press release or news release to grab an editor's or station manager's attention. We'll look at the press release later in this chapter and talk about the purpose, structure, and tone that you must have in order for you press release to work. But before we get there, I want to point out that traditional media outlets – TV, radio, and print – aren't the only media platforms in today's digital world. You can also appear on someone else's podcast or YouTube channel. While these may not seem as credible or effective, they can be just as profitable if you leverage them properly. We'll explore "leveraging your authority" in Chapter 20. For now, let's look at the second type of media platform...

Your Own Media Platform

Throughout history, people have created their own media platforms to reach the target audience they wanted to reach. An extreme example is Dr. John Brinkley, who in 1930 started his own radio station just over the U.S. border in Mexico to reach people from all over the world and offer them alternative medical solutions. If you've never heard of Dr. John Brinkley, look him up and read about how he sold goat testicles for male impotency. I should point out that he's an interesting person to study too for his marketing prowess. Yes, he was a bit shady and a borderline criminal (the U.S. government banned him from the radio in the 1920's, which is the reason he built his own station in Mexico), but the core of what he did was fascinating, and you could probably learn a thing or two from his tactics.

Anyway, that's an extreme example. In today's business environment, entrepreneurs create their own media platforms with iTunes, YouTube, and a whole host of other digital platforms that allow them to create and host audio or video podcasts, online TV channels, etc. There's no reason you can't do the same thing and create your own media platform where you talk about whatever you want and/or interview people in your niche who can help your ideal, target audience. I think this goes without saying, but I'll say it anyway: like creating your own stage for speaking, creating your own media platform will take a lot of work and can be very time consuming. That's not to say you couldn't or shouldn't take the time. Done right, creating your own media platform can position you as an authority fast and bring in tons of new business. That's for you to decide.

Personally, I've done both. I've been on other people's media platforms – TV, radio, print, and podcasts – and I've created my own media platforms. They are completely different animals, and both have unique pros and cons. For example, being on someone else's media platform takes persistence and luck. About a decade ago now, when I owned my fitness business, I put out a press release every week for over a year. I pitched exercise ideas. I pitched nutrition ideas. I pitched everything I could think of.

Want to know what got picked up first, after a year of persistence? Yellow tomatoes. Yep, I pitched a plethora of fantastic ideas, but a local radio station picked up my press release on yellow tomatoes and how they have more potassium than bananas. I was excited to be on the radio, but I was dumbfounded as to why they chose that topic over the others I sent in.

So, the point is, one major con with being on someone else's media platform is you never know what will get picked up. Media outlets are starving for your information. But you just never know what they're going to choose. I despise that aspect of other media platforms, but that's the nature of the beast.

Actually, that's one reason why I decided to create my own media platform years later. I didn't want to deal with the B.S., so I created my own podcast to get the information out to the public without waiting on other media platforms to pick it up. That's a pro of creating your own platform. You have complete control. But reach (or number of viewers) is a big con to your own platform and a pro for someone else's platform. TV station reach tens of thousands, hundreds of thousands, even millions of viewers. Your new podcast or YouTube channel, while it has the potential to reach that many people, probably won't for a long time. Again, like anything else, there are pros and cons to each.

Now that you know the two types of media platforms, let's look at the three traditional ways to get noticed by someone else's media platform. First, like I mentioned earlier, you can contact media outlets yourself by using a press release.

Press Release

A press release or a news release is simply a document that tells the media outlet what you propose to talk about and how that information will be welcomed by their audience. The press release can be mailed, faxed, or emailed to the contact person. Every point person is different in how he or she likes to receive the press releases. Your first job is to find out who the point person/contact person is. Your second job is to find out which press release method they prefer so you can reach out to them in the most effective way possible.

So, how do you find the right person to contact? It's easy. All you have to do is look at the directory on their website or in their material if they're a print media. You can even call the media outlet and ask who you need to send your press release to. They'll ask you a little about your topic and give you the correct contact person's information. It's that easy. And once you have the point person's contact information, just ask him or her which method – mail, fax, or email – he prefers.

As you can see, the easiest part of this process is finding the point of contact. Instead, what you'll find out is that the hardest part of this process – at least the most time-consuming

> The media is always looking for quality content for their audience.

part – is choosing which media outlet to contact and which department to send your press release to. This will take time and patience on your end. Sending your press release to the right contact gives you a chance at getting media attention. Sending your press release to the wrong contact person ensures that you won't get any media attention, and you'll end up pissing off the contact person you have because your ideas have nothing to do with his department.

You have to understand that these people are busy and stressed. Yes, they are always looking for quality content for their audience. But they are always on a deadline and in need of the right information, right now.

Let me give you a quick example about the correct media outlet. Let's say you're a massage therapist. Your city's alternative health or natural health media outlets will most likely be your first choice. Sending your press release to the business media outlets would most likely be a waste of time for you and that media outlet. That's not to say you couldn't spin your content to fit another market. You can, and we'll discuss that in the next chapter. But in most cases, you'll want to stick to your topic's and profession's most-likely-to-succeed media outlets.

In the next chapter, I'll show you how to write your press release. For now, let's move on to the second way to get noticed by someone else's media platform: using a press release service, like PR News Wire.

A Press Release Service

If you're interested, you can google "press release services" to get a list of these companies. Sending press releases yourself is free. These services require an investment. Some of the investments are small, some are ridiculous, some are a la carte, and some are monthly fees. The main benefit to services like these are that they already have the list of media outlets you want to send you press release to. This benefit can greatly shortcut your time and effort because they have the lists you want, and they send to the correct contact people for your topics all the time. But again, there's a cost to doing business with these services. You must decide if you want to go the cheaper route (i.e. doing it yourself) or just get it done.

When I first started out, I went the cheaper route and took care of all my press releases myself. There's nothing wrong with doing it that way, especially if you have a knack for writing press releases that get picked up by the media. But you'll never know if you have that skill unless you try. Using these services takes a lot of the guess work out of the process and can speed up your success. You may find these services beneficial, especially if all you're after is manufacturing your own authority.

What do I mean by manufacturing your own authority? Well, when we're talking about traditional media, being in the media has two major benefits. The main benefit is appearing in the media: on TV, on the radio, in print, on a YouTube channel, or on a podcast. But the secondary benefit is way more powerful, and that benefit is how you leverage your media appearance after the fact and how you can really grow your authority fast.

You see, I've been on TV, on the radio, in print, and on multiple podcasts, and I can tell you from personal experience that your phone isn't ringing off the hook after appearing in the media. Most people think that's what happens. It doesn't. Sure, you may get a couple calls from people who are interested in what you had to say and want to do business with you, but that's not the norm for most media outlets.

Remember, you don't get in the media to sell anything. Your whole goal is to educate the media outlet's audience. And what that does for you is help you position and establish yourself as an authority. That's the real reason you want to be in the media.

Now, do you remember when we talked about perception being reality and how you don't have to be an authority to be seen as an authority? Well, by simply getting into the media in some fashion, you're able to tell people you've been in the media. And that's what you're really after anyway. So for example, if you use a media service and a media outlet places your press release or proposal on their website, then technically you've appeared in their media. Your being in the media verifiable and the whole world can see your press release, so it's legit.

What does that mean for you? If you use a service like PRLeads.com, you can have them send your press release out to hundreds of media outlets. And the way their particular system works is that they guarantee at least 50 outlets will pick up your story. No, 50 outlets won't call you for an interview, put you on the radio, have you on TV, or anything like that. But 50 outlets will place your press release on their websites. So, what does that do for you? This kind of coverage allows you to use those media outlets' logos on your website, in your print material, on your business card, and anywhere else you want to position yourself as an authority.

Now, I know what some of you are thinking? That sounds like cheating. Well, some would call this tactic cheating. Others would call it effectively and efficiently using your time. Listen, getting into the media is not easy. And if all you're really after is establishing yourself as an authority to your ideal, target audience, then using a service like this to manufacture your authority is totally cool in my book. After all, you really appeared in the media. Your appearance may not be a "traditional" approach but it's not a lie. It's the truth. And by using the media outlets' logos and names, your target audience will perceive you as an authority.

Now, if you're goal is not just to appear in the media but actually get into the media on a regular basis, then these first two ways may be useful. But the third way may be your best option. The third way to use someone else's media platform is by hiring a...

Publicist

This is the most expensive way to get into the media, but you may find this option the most beneficial if your goal is to appear on major media outlets and get media attention repeatedly.

Publicists are professional media connectors. Their job is to establish relationships with media outlets and media contacts and pitch ideas that will benefit the media's audience. In other words, they're the middle men (or women) between you and the media. They'll listen to your ideas and help you craft the perfect message for the specific media outlet you want to get into. They'll then take your idea and pitch it to the media contacts they have relationships with.

Sometimes they knock the pitch out of the park and get you on TV, the radio, etc. fast. Other times, they fail to do so and come back to you to get more ideas. This is a process and can take time and patience. This process is no different than anything else worthy of your time. So, if you choose to go this route, have the correct mindset before investing your time and money.

I have a story for you that illustrates the unpredictable nature of publicists. My friend, Collin Stover, has been in the *Pittsburgh City Paper* (on the front cover) and in a few other media outlets, including *Whirl Magazine*. His *City Paper* experience is one of luck. He was contacted by the media because they were doing their own story idea on magicians (the business he owned at the time) and he was the only magician to show up at the photo shoot. So, with a little persuasion, he landed his first media appearance on the cover. Pure luck. And he'll tell you that himself. In fact, when he and I teach positioning tactics together, he tells that story and how it's never happened again.

So, how did he get into *Whirl Magazine*? He hired a publicist. And as luck would have it, his publicist was able to take his idea and get him a featured story in that magazine. People try for months and years to do what he did. But his publicist's relationship with the media contact, the spin they put on the idea, and the timing of it all is what made that feature story happen within a relatively short period of time.

Okay, now that you know the two types of media platforms and the three ways to use someone else's media platform, let's look at how you can…

Use Your Own Media Platform to Manufacture Your Authority

First, like we briefly talked about before, you can start your own podcast or YouTube channel to manufacture your own authority. You can talk about whatever you want, or you can invite guests on to be interviewed by you. Personally, I enjoy interviewing other experts. These interviews can be time-consuming to set up and execute, but there are some incredible benefits. The major one being that your audience sees you as an authority if you're interviewing other authorities. Think Oprah, Bill O'Reilly, and any other host that interviews guests.

Another major benefit to the interview model is being able to talk to these other authorities and celebrities without any

> "You can manufacture your own authority by interviewing other authorities."

hassles. Think about this opportunity. If you were in the music business and you want to chat it up with your favorite artist, how do you think the conversation would go if you called him out of the blue? Probably not good. But if you're in the media and want to interview him about his new album, how do you think he'd respond to the offer of being interviewed? In most cases, he'd be thrilled.

So as you can see, getting other authorities for interviews on your media outlet is just a matter of positioning. In the first scenario, you're a creepy fan. In the second scenario, you're a host and can get them into the media. Granted, your own media outlet may be small, but it's media nonetheless. And most people are thrilled to be interviewed.

Okay, so what if you don't want to start your own podcast or YouTube channel? You can still manufacture your own authority by rigging an interview. Remember, perception is reality. So in reality, whoever interviews you doesn't really matter.

Yes, being interviewed by a TV show host would be better, but you can get a friend to interview you, make the content available to prospects, and position yourself as an authority in less than a week. Seriously. I've done this myself and for my clients. It's easy. All you have to do is find a friend or business associate who can speak well and who is willing to interview you. Then, create a list of questions that you want to answer. Practice a little before the interview. And finally, jump on the phone and record a phone interview. The interviewer doesn't even have to mention where he's from. He simply starts with, "Welcome to today's call, on the line we have so and so..." and then have him read a short bio about you. He can then can launch into the questions you've provided, and you can answer away.

Like any interview, keep calm and relaxed and have fun. Then, once you're done with the interview, upload the MP3 to Amazon AWS or a service like Audio Acrobat, and post the content on your website or place the link in your email sequence to prospects. If you're really ambitious, you can turn the MP3 into a CD or flash drive that you can physically mail to prospects.

We've cover a lot in this chapter. And before we move on to one of the most important subjects in this book – leveraging your authority – I want to circle back to the press release and give you some more detail on how to write a press release. In the next chapter, we'll look at the four areas of focus when writing a press release.

> "To hell with circumstances;
> I create opportunities."
>
> ~Bruce Lee

19

Writing Your Press Release

There are four areas of focus you'll want to pay attention to when you write a press release:

1. Purpose
2. Structure
3. Tone
4. Spin

Purpose of the Press Release

The purpose of your press release is two-fold: a. grab the contact person's attention and b. demonstrate your authority. Remember, you're not the only person sending a press release to the media contact. The contact person probably receive dozens, some may be hundreds, of press releases every, single day.

These people are busy and on a deadline. You have to grab their attention immediately. How do you do that? That leads us to the…

Structure of the Press Release

The first way to grab attention is to have an attention-grabbing headline that tells a story in one sentence. Your title must be big, bold, and near the top of the page. It can be direct. It can be intriguing. But it must not be salesy. "Salesy" kills your press release. The media is not interested in selling you or your products and services. Their only purpose is to serve their audience. Not you. This is huge and something we'll talk about in a minute when we look at the tone of your press release.

As for your headline, there's no time to mess around here. Get straight to the point. This is your only chance at grabbing their attention. Why? Because with so many press releases coming in and deadlines looming over their heads, the contact people read the headlines first. If your title doesn't strike their interest immediately, then they throw your press release away and never read any more. It sucks but that's the nature of the beast. Like I've said several times, these people are busy, they have deadlines, and they have plenty of people sending them ideas.

Now, here's the thing, if your headline grabs the contact person's attention, they'll read your opening paragraph. This paragraph tells the entire story. The what, when, how, and who. You have three to four sentences to give all the details they need to make a decision. Remember, the contact person is reading your press release with one mission in mind. Is this news my audience wants to hear? That's it. If your press release doesn't present news that his audience is interested in and finds relevant, then he'll toss your press release without a second thought.

By the way, those words should sound familiar: interesting and relevant. That's all any audience is looking for. Is it relevant to me? "Yes, then I'll read some more." "No, then I'm not wasting my time." Is it interesting to me? "Yes, then I'll continue reading." "No, then I'm done with this… I don't have time for anything boring."

If you're opening paragraph does its job, then the next paragraph or two can give some more insight into the idea you're pitching to the media. Bullet points can work well too. And I think including quotes from you here is important as well. Why? Because this is where you can start to demonstrate your authority. Experts are quoted, so when you put your own words in quotes you demonstrate that you're an expert.

The final paragraph tells the contact person who you are and why you're qualified to be on their media platform. If you're an author, then lead with that detail. If you've been in business a long time, then say that. If you've helped thousands of people, then say that too. However, while you want to demonstrate your authority, it's important to keep the right tone. So, let's look at the…

Tone of the Press Release

The tone of the press release must not be salesy. You're not trying to sell anything here. You're simply giving the contact people information and news that their audience may want to know. That's why your tone must be set in the third person. Personally, I write better in first person, where I talk directly to the reader. Maybe that's why most of my press releases never got picked up. Writing in third person means that you're writing the press release from an outside perspective. So, instead of saying, "Over the past 17 years, **I've** helped thousands of coaches… ." You have to say, "Over the past 17 years, **Weston Lyon** has helped thousands of coaches… ."

Also, remember that you're not necessarily talking to the media contact people here. Instead, you're telling them what their audience wants to hear. Remember, their goal is to serve their audience. If they don't think you have their audience's best interest at heart, then they won't hesitate to toss your press release. Your tone must be from an outside perspective, and your tone must give their audience great information that's newsworthy. Okay, the last area for press releases I want us to look at is…

Spin

There are two ways to look at "spin." First, think about making your idea unique. Being unique is important no matter what we're doing. Earlier in this book, we talked a lot about you being unique to your audience. When we're talking about the media, it's just as important that your ideas are unique. That's not to say you can't talk about the same topic as someone else. You can. But the more unique you can make the topic, the more spin you put on the topic, the more likely the media will pick up your topic.

Honestly, I think that's the only reason my yellow tomato idea got any traction. Like I mentioned earlier, for over a year, I sent tons of great ideas to the media, but the first idea they picked up on was yellow tomatoes having more potassium than bananas. The spin I put on that was all about athletes eating bananas for their potassium content but how there are other fruits and vegetables that are better than bananas. The yellow tomato idea was unique. While other trainers were telling the media's audience to eat bananas, I was telling them to look at other fruits and vegetables that are even better, like yellow tomatoes. You want to make your ideas unique too by putting some type of spin on your topic.

The other way to look at spin is to look at how you can take an average topic for your regular audience and create a whole new idea for a completely different audience. For example, if we go back to the massage therapy example we talked about earlier, we could spin a press release about wrist pain like this…

For general news stations, we could talk about wrist pain and gardening in the spring or wrist pain and snow shoveling in the winter. You see, wrist pain is the topic, and the time of year and what people are doing is the spin. News channels and radio stations may eat that up if you send out your press

> The goal of the media is to serve their audience, not sell your products and services.

release at the right time. In fact, some media outlets have an editorial calendar that they share on their website. If they have a calendar like this, get that calendar and study what topics are important when. You can create your own calendar to coincide with their calendar so you're always sending ideas that match with what the contact people are looking for. Very smart.

Okay, let's look at this example some more. You could take that same topic (wrist pain) with the same spin (wrist pain and gardening), and you could target niche magazines or newsletters that focus on gardening. You're not writing anything new. You're simply putting a unique spin on the topic. See how that works?

We've covered a lot over the last six chapters, and you now know the three ways to demonstrate your authority for your audience and become Authority-Present: write a book, be a speaker, and be in the media. In the next chapter, we're going to look how you can leverage your authority.

20

Leveraging Your Authority

Writing a book, becoming a speaker, and getting into the media will position you as an authority in your field faster than any of other marketing strategies or tactics available. However, while demonstrating your authority is the key to being authority-present in the mind of your audience, you won't get nearly as far and succeed as much unless you learn to leverage your authority. That's why in this chapter, we're going to look at five ways to start leveraging your authority in your marketing material and place of business.

Leverage Point #1: In Your Office or Store

YOUR BOOK ON DISPLAY

If you're an author, having your book on display in your office or store is a great way to leverage your authority. After all, if people don't know you're an author, then being an author isn't effectively positioning you as an authority. That's why showing off what you've done is important. Having your book on display allows people to see you're an author and ask you questions about the writing process or about your book.

PICTURES WITH OTHER AUTHORITIES & CELEBRITIES

A second way to leverage your authority at your office is to have pictures of you on your wall with other celebrities. We'll talk more about images and symbols of success in Chapter 25, but for now understand that when you're seen with other authorities and celebrities, their authority and/or celebrity rubs off on you in the mind of the person seeing the pictures.

Here's a picture with me and James Malinchak. James is a celebrity in the marketing world and was featured on the ABC's hit TV show, Secret Millionaire. People in my niche know him and respect him. And when they see me with him at his house, they always ask about the story. This picture positions me as an authority alongside James and allows me to further position myself and leverage my authority by talking about how I ended up at James' house, how I'm a speaker, and much more.

PICTURES OF YOU ON STAGE OR IN THE MEDIA

A third way to leverage your authority at your office is to have pictures of you on stage or in the media. If you've been on stage, then showing yourself on stage is a great way to strike up a conversation about your experience as a speaker.

The same goes for you being on TV, in a magazine, or any other media outlet you've appeared in. If you've been in print media, then framing the newspaper article or magazine cover for all visitors to see is a great way to leverage your authority. If you've been on TV, then an image of you on TV is a way to leverage your authority. Or maybe you've been on TV or on the radio and you have a picture of you with the host. Again, pictures allow you to leverage your authority and tell stories about your experience. As you already know, perception is reality. Images and pictures of you on stage, with other celebrities, and in the media, go a long way with your target audience's perception of you.

Look at the pictures on the next page. If you had these types of pictures of you in the media, imagine the impact these would have on your prospects when they walked into your office or place of business.

A client and me on KDKA TV

My client, Kathy Parry, on Fox News 8

TESTIMONIALS EVERYWHERE

A fourth and final way to leverage your authority at your office is to have testimonials laid out everywhere. We'll talk about testimonials and what others say about you starting in Chapter 21, but for now understand that testimonials in your office are another great way to leverage your authority. They

My friend and referral partner, Collin Stover, on the cover of the *Pittsburgh City Paper*

can be framed and placed on your wall. They can be laminated and placed on your desk or on a waiting room table. You can even place them in a picture book and have a book of testimonials for all visitors to look at while they're waiting for you. Testimonials speak volumes about you and your authority.

Moving out of your physical office and online, the next place to leverage your authority is...

Leverage Point #2: On Your Website

Listen, if you don't have a website, you need one. And while you're at it, I recommend getting an email address connected to your website, so you have a more professional email address. There's nothing that screams amateur as much as a Gmail, Yahoo, or Hotmail email address. Web domains and web hosting are less than $200 a year. Make the investment and upgrade your online game right now. As for leveraging your authority on your website, there are several things you'll want to do...

YOUR HOME PAGE

First, you want to make sure your website visitors know that you're an author, speaker, and media personality. To do that, you'll want to find a way to work in your book, images of you on stage, and images of you in the media (or media brands and icons) on your Home Page.

For example, here's my friend, Collin Stover, again. As you can see (bottom of image), Collin has media brands and icons on his home page that show you what media he's appeared in.

Here's another example, this time from the man who inspired me to get into the fitness business over a decade ago, Matt Furey. As you can see, Matt has some of his books on his home page, as well as magazine covers he's appeared on over the years. If you had any doubt about his authority position before getting to his site, these images put that doubt to rest and demonstrate to you that he's the real deal.

YOUR ABOUT PAGE

Another place on your website to leverage your authority is on your "About Page." Your About Page is a great catch-all page that you can tell your story and place as many images as you want.

On the next page, you'll see some examples from my About Page. Notice how I use my About Page to not only tell you my story – struggle, transition, and success – but to show off images of me with other celebrities that I want my prospect to see.

Stop Prospecting And Start Positioning
An Entrepreneurial Story About Fear, Love, & Passion

I remember the exact moment I decided to write my first book. I was on a flight to the west coast for a business trip, and I was reading a chapter in Dan Kennedy's *No BS Sales Success* book called "Positioning, Not Prospecting."

In the chapter, Dan talks about how you can position yourself as an expert and a leading authority in your field so prospects come to you instead of you going to them.

I related to the chapter title even before reading the content of the chapter. You see, I started my entrepreneurial career in the multi-level marketing (MLM) industry, where we 'prospected' to get customers and distributors.

I really learned a lot in that industry. From my experiences, I built a solid foundation of sales and marketing experience, as well as developed a thick skin, impervious to criticism.

Start your About Page with an interesting story (above) and be sure to share some authority-positioning pictures (below).

About Weston Lyon

Weston Lyon is the author of 18 books and one of the only authors to ever write 9 books in 11 months. In addition, Weston is the Founder of Plug & Play Publishing – a Pittsburgh-based information marketing company that teaches coaches, consultants, speakers, and other service providers how to position themselves as authorities in their fields, persuade prospects to become clients, and grow their businesses using back-end profit centers.

When Weston is not working, he's enjoying life with his son, family, or friends, training in an array of martial arts, or out on the mountain bike trails.

- Weston Teaching Authority Positioning Strategies to Local Business Owners
- Weston with 34.5 Million Woman, Becky Auer
- Weston with Millionaire-Maker, Dan Kennedy
- Weston with Celebrity Entrepreneur, James Malinchak
- Weston Lyon with "I Love Marketing" Host, Joe Polish
- Weston with the Founder of BNI, Dr. Ivan Misner
- Weston at a martial arts training
- Weston getting ready to race with Yanik Silver and crew
- Weston with his son on the mountain bike trails

For instance, in the bottom image on page 162, you'll notice me on stage as well as with other celebrities in my field. In addition, you may also notice that I have images that show off my personality too. As you can see, I'm showing you my other passions: martial arts, adventure seeking, and mountain biking. Remember we talked about becoming interesting to your target audience. These types of pictures show another side of you and make you interesting to your audience. They also serve as trust and relationship-building tools. For example, a fellow martial artist who sees this image will immediately feel a level of trust with me. The same goes for any adventure seeker or parent since I include my son in the last image. Never underestimate the power of pictures and stories. The more you show and the more you tell, the more trust you build.

NOTE: I understand the images may be difficult to see the finer details, especially if your eyes are like mine. So, if you'd like a bigger, better view of my About Page please visit: PlugAndPlayPublishing.com/about.

On page 164, you'll see a couple of the images up close. Take a quick peek now before reading the next paragraph.

Now, do you notice anything else with these images? I've placed a caption under each picture. Captions are another, wonderful way to build trust and establish authority on your website. Captions are simple to implement but have a profound effect on your audience's perception.

If you visit my About Page, you'll notice that the captions allow me to tell you who I'm with and a little about the peo-

Weston with the Founder of BNI,
Dr. Ivan Misner

Weston getting ready to race with
Yanik Silver and crew

ple I feature. But that's not all captions can do. I can also tell you a story with captions. Here are three such examples...

Susan Frantz, a retired high school teacher, who has leveraged her book to create an annual five-figure, part-time income serving universities and students...

Kathy Parry, a "real food" coach and speaker, who has positioned her book and story to the media to leverage media appearance after media appearance...

Fred Liesong & Charlie Hauck, owners of a sales performance organization, who have used their book to generate $149,456 from their first tradeshow after being published...

On the left: Susan Frantz, a retired high school teacher, who has leveraged her book to create an annual five-figure, part-time income serving universities and students.

In the middle: Kathy Parry, a "real food" coach and speaker, who has positioned her book and story in the media to leverage media appearance after media appearance.

On the right: Fred Liesong & Charlie Hauck, owners of a sales performance organization, who have used their book to generate $149,456 at their very first tradeshow after being published.

As you can see, one sentence allows me to tell you the main highlights I want you to know. Captions are very powerful if used correctly.

YOUR SUCCESS STORIES PAGE

Another place on your website to leverage your authority is on your Success Stories Page. Just like having testimonials throughout your office, testimonials on your website allow you to leverage your authority and instantly build trust with your visitors. You can do this on a Success Stories Page, a page completely dedicated to testimonials.

The best example I've ever seen with this tactic is Matt Furey's testimonial page (www.mattfurey.com/testimonials). The testimonials are endless. See for yourself. When you get to the page, click the down arrow on the right side of your browser and count how long you take to reach the bottom of the page. I counted over twenty seconds to reach the bottom. Think about that. You arrive on his page and start reading the first few testimonials. You then start scrolling down the page and take another fifteen seconds to reach the bottom.

What's going through your head while you're experiencing this? I can tell you from personal experience, this is exactly what I did over a decade ago when I found his success stories page: I read the first three testimonials and then started scrolling. After seeing dozens and dozens of testimonials flash by my eyes, I decided I didn't even need to read any more. I rationalized that if he had this many testimonials, he must be damn good and the authority on the topic of fitness.

If you have a list of testimonials, your prospects will feel the same way. Again, we'll cover testimonials and the power of what others say about you starting in Chapter 21. For now, leverage your authority by placing testimonials on your website.

One last, quick point about testimonials on your website: you don't have to have an entire page dedicated to testimonials. If you have enough to fill out an entire page, then having an entire page dedicated to testimonials a smart strategy. But it's not essential. You can still leverage your authority by using just a handful of testimonials on your Home Page, your About Page, your Sales Pages, and any other page you want to.

And they don't have to be new testimonials either. If you have a handful of testimonials, (four to five will suffice) you can place two to three on your Home Page, another two to three on your Sales Pages, and the same exact ones (this time in a different order) on your About Page, and you'll be good to go. The quality of the testimonials matters much more than the quantity.

Leverage Point #3: In Your Email Signature

The next place you can leverage your authority is in your emails. This is an easy option. Every email system has the ability to create a custom signature. You can leverage your authority in every single email you send out by creating a custom signature that demonstrates your authority.

For example, a client of mine, Pete Gradowski's email looks like this…

Pete Gradowski
Owner, Pete G. Magic
Author of the *The Birthday Party Planning Guide*
XXX-XXX-XXXX
Email@Email.com

Learn how to throw the most incredible birthday party for your child and create a moment they'll never forget. Get my book today and only pay shipping.

As you can see, the email signature has his name and his position: Owner, Pete G. Magic. But it also has "Author of the *The Birthday Party Planning Guide*" and "Learn how to throw the most incredible birthday party for your children and create a moment they'll never forget. Get my book today and only pay shipping."

Not only does Pete let his email recipients know that he's an author, he also offers them his book for free. This is a simple, yet powerful strategy for leveraging your authority. After all, how many emails do you send? I'm betting over a hundred a month, at least. That's over a thousand emails per year. Demonstrating and leveraging your authority over a thousand times per year helps you cement your expertise in other people's minds.

Remember, you don't need to be an author to do this either. You can show off the media brands and icons from where you've appeared or you can steer people online to watch one of your speeches. Whatever you're doing to demonstrate your authority, make sure you duplicate that strategy in your email signature.

Leverage Point #4: On Your Business Card

How many business cards do you give away each year? Hundreds? Thousands? I think you get the point. Leveraging your authority on your business card is a very smart way to get the message out that you're the expert and that you're the person your target audience should be doing business with. Let me give you two examples of my own business cards.

FRONT   BACK

This first one (above) is a blast from the past. This business card is circa 2007-ish when I owned my fitness business. Can you identify the two ways I demonstrated my authority?

First, I have a testimonial on the back of the card from a client. Yes, you can use testimonials on your business cards too. In fact, you can use testimonials anywhere and everywhere. And I highly recommend you do use testimonials when you have them.

The second tactic is my book cover. By having my book cover on my business card, you know that I'm an author and an authority on my topic. You can do the same. If you're an author, put your book cover on your business card. If you're a speaker, put an image of you on stage on your business card. If you've been in the media, put the media outlet's brands or names on your business card.

Now, a word of warning. Business cards are small, so you don't want everything on your card. Instead, you'll want to choose the most impactful authority symbol you have. If you're an author, your book cover will most likely be the most powerful. But, again, use whatever you have and leverage your authority as best you can.

Okay, one last thing about this business card that you may find interesting. With my graphic designer at the time, we designed and developed a series of business cards like the one featured above that we modeled after trading cards. Yep, the card you see here with me doing a handstand, is just one of four cards I had with me at networking events that I handed out to people. I'd joke around by telling people that they could "collect all four" by meeting me at different events.

FRONT

BACK

Be creative with your marketing material and figure out simple ways to stand out to your audience. A little creativity can go a long way.

This next business card (above) is newer. As you can see, this card is not as elaborate as my old one, but it does the job just fine. Can you identify where I demonstrate my authority? Pretty simple right? I demonstrate my authority on the back where I show off my book cover. I kept this card a little cleaner than the last one, but like I said, it does the job just fine. Remember, don't make this complicated. Simply demonstrate your authority and let your audience's mind do the rest. Their minds will fill in the blanks, and they'll jump to their own conclusion with just a little help from you.

Leverage Point #5: In Your Advertisements

The last place I want to talk about in this chapter to leverage your authority is in your advertisements. Yes, your ads are meant to sell – whether that's getting someone to take an offer for free or getting them to give you money – so you don't want to waste any space. However, making sales are all about getting people to trust you. And the best way to get people to trust you is to position yourself as an authority.

So, demonstrating your authority in your ads whenever and wherever you can is important. How can you accomplish these demonstrations? By doing the same things we've talked about throughout this chapter. If you're an author, show your book cover. If you're a speaker, show an image of you speaking. If you've been in the media, show yourself in the media. If you have testimonials, share your testimonials. Again, the whole point of leveraging your authority is to demonstrate your authority everywhere you can with whatever you can.

Now, you need make the ad, email, business card, or whatever look good and professional. But you also want to sprinkle your authority symbols into these places where you can. Yes, it's a balancing act, but learning to leverage your authority in all these places will help you grow your business by positioning yourself as an authority, sticking out in a crowded sea of competitors, and showing your ideal audience that you're the only person they should consider doing business with.

I recommend taking some time now to create an inventory of what you have. Do you have a book? Do you have images of you speaking on stage? Have you appeared in the media? Do you have testimonials? Inventory the ways you can demonstrate and then leverage your authority by implementing the tactics in this chapter.

Be Talkable

We've covered a lot of ground so far. So, for your convenience, let's recap what you've learned thus far. First, you learned that you don't have to be an authority yet to be perceived as an authority. With the right intention, you can ethically position yourself as an authority and start helping your ideal, target audience right now. Next, you learned that you must do what real authorities do and behave how real authorities behave to be perceived as a real authority. If you don't, then people won't *see* you as an authority – even if you *are* a real authority. Then, you learned the first three steps in my five-step formula to help you quickly establish trust, confidence, and a powerful, authority position…

Step 1: Be Relevant

In Step One, you learned that you must be relevant to your ideal, target audience. And to be relevant, you have to know, understand, empathize, and talk about the situations they're currently experiencing: what fears they are trying avoid; what desires they are trying to achieve; what drivers they value most; and what motives they rely on to move them forward and help them transition from their current situation to a new, ideal situation (i.e. helping them go from where they are to where they want to be).

Step 2: Be Interesting

In Step Two, you learned that once you grab your audience's attention with relevant content, you must make your message interesting and unique. And the easiest way to make your message unique is by making yourself interesting and unique and by creating a better version of yourself to show the world. We call that new, better version of you your unique Authority Character. You also learned how you can best relate to your ideal audience by telling them how you struggled with some aspect of your life, how you transitioned out of your struggle by finding a better way, and how you ultimately succeeded in some way, shape, or form.

Those three components (struggle, transition, success) are called your backstory, and you learned how to tell someone your backstory in one sentence as well as when to give them more details about your backstory. You also learned that there are Heroic Qualities you want your target audience to know about you and Dark-Side Tendencies that you want to tone down so your audience sees you as a real person and not some perfect, fake authority. And you also learned that audiences follow leaders and authorities like you because of the philosophy you have – who you are, what you stand for, and what you're aggressively against.

Step 3: Be Authority-Present

In Step Three, you learned that authorities are seen as authorities because of where their messages appear – in books, on stages, and in the media – and that you must appear in the same places if you want to fully demonstrate your authority and become authority-present. In addition, you learned the first steps to help you start writing a book, the different types of stages you can speak from, the different types of speeches you can give, and the formula for creating an unforgettable speech. You also learned the different types of media you can get into, the three ways to get into traditional media, and how to manufacture your own authority. And finally, you learned about the five places you can begin to leverage your authority and get your ideal, target audience to see you as an authority.

That's what you've learned so far. Over the next several chapters, we're going to explore Step Four…

Be Talkable

We now want to shift the focus away from you and start looking at what others say about you. In other words, we want to become "talkable" – getting others to talk about us so we can further strengthen our authority position in the marketplace and convert more prospects into clients. How are we going to get people talking about us?

First, we're going to look at testimonials and endorsements, and I'm going to show you how you can elicit the best testimonials from your current and past clients. Then, we're going to explore the best types of referrals, how people talk about you when they refer you, and how you can make it easier for clients, associates, colleagues, and friends to refer you more business.

If implemented correctly, these next several chapters can completely change your business. You're going to love them!

21

Demonstrating Your Authority with Testimonials and Endorsements

In this chapter, we're going to look at testimonials and endorsements: what they are, what makes them effective, and how to get as many as you can, so you can demonstrate your authority in a powerful, non-threatening way and leverage your authority in as many places as possible.

So, what are testimonials and endorsements, and how are they different from each other? In my opinion, a testimonial is a third-party opinion of how you've helped the person giving the testimonial. For instance, a perfect testimonial for my last book, *The Most Powerful Business Tool Ever to Exist*, would be:

> "This book is amazing! It showed me exactly what a book could do for my business and helped me get over some of the fears I was having. I'm happy to say that I've started writing my own book."

An endorsement, on the other hand, is a third-party opinion of how you help your audience in general. And more often than not, an endorsement is given by another authority or celebrity in your field who you may or may not have helped. For example, Dr. Ivan Misner, the founder of BNI said this about the same book I referenced above:

> "In this powerful book, Weston shows you that a book is not only the best business card you can have but how a book is also the best business tool for generating referrals, converting sales, and acquiring customers, clients and patients for your company."

The first example is a testimonial. It is an opinion about how I helped the reader. The second example is an endorsement. It is an opinion about how my book will help the other readers of the book.

Understanding the power of both testimonials and endorsements is important. After all, depending on the relationship you have with your prospects and the trust you've built with them, they may not always believe what you say (yet). If your prospects already know you and like you, then getting them to trust you is easier, and an effective testimonial or endorsement could send prospects over the edge to trust you enough to buy from you. If prospects don't know you or like you yet, an effective testimonial or endorsement could get them to like you more and get them to start trusting you. As you know, trust is the first step in the buying process and why we want to position ourselves as authorities in the first place. People trust authorities, and testimonials and endorsements help us demonstrate our authority in a different way than writing a book, becoming a speaker, or appearing in the media does.

So, what makes a testimonial or endorsement good or bad, effective or ineffective? The number one factor is specificity. When your testimonials and endorsements are specific, they are seen as authentic. And when they come across as authentic, they strike a chord with your audience and create trust. So the more specific your testimonials and endorsements are, the more authentic they appear and the more effective and powerful they are.

Regarding testimonials specifically, there are three types of effective testimonials:

1. Results-Oriented Testimonials
2. Objection-Covering Testimonials
3. Failure Turnaround Testimonials

Results-Oriented Testimonials

Results-Oriented Testimonials are testimonials that share a specific result that was achieved. For example, one of my clients came back from a tradeshow and told me that his com-

> When your testimonials and endorsements are specific, they are seen as authentic.

pany generated $149,456 in sales using his newly written book as a tool. That was a fantastic result. And a specific result. So, I use that testimonial in many places because it is both amazing and specific.

But results don't have to be based on money or return on investment. If you own a fitness business, helping a client lose seventeen pounds in three weeks is results-oriented. If you're a financial coach, helping a client eliminate $19,873 of debt in 29 months is results-oriented. I think you get the point. Whatever result your audience wants, you want to have testimonials that are based on those results, and you want to be as specific as possible.

Objection-Covering Testimonials

Objection-Covering Testimonials help you cover objections that your audience is having. I will tell you that most business owners fail to use these types of testimonials. However, these testimonials offer you an extremely powerful way for you to build trust and authority fast. Let me give you an example. Let's say you're a dating coach for entrepreneurial men who are recently divorced. An objection-covering testimonial could sound like this, "I'm a business owner who travels a lot for work, so meeting women in my home town is very hard. Well, at least finding dates was hard until I found Don Juan. Don has helped me change my mindset about dating as well as helped me come up with a great way to meet someone just like me. I'm excited to get out there and find someone new."

You see, this testimonial has nothing to do with results. The client hasn't gotten results yet. But this testimonial is still excellent because it covers an objection these men have: I don't know if you can help me find someone because I'm so busy. This testimonial helps eliminate that objection without you saying a word. The third-party testimonial does all the heavy lifting for you and establishes you as the authority on the matter.

Failure Turnaround Testimonials

Failure Turnaround Testimonials are when you have a failure or a perceived failure that could be harmful to your business, and you let the testimonial giver show your audience how you turned the situation all around and gave great customer service.

For example, a past client of mine who is in the interior decorating business had a testimonial that stated, "We had a glitch with our remote window shades, but Kathleen's 'No Risk, No Problem Guarantee' took care of everything. Her installer came to the house and fixed the issue – free of charge! A wonderful team to work with from start to finish!"

This testimonial is pure gold because it shows the audience how much her company values customer service and how her clients have nothing to worry about, even if something goes wrong.

Limiting or eliminating your audience's risk is another way to position yourself as the go-to guy or gal. Risk can kill trust and therefore a sale. Experts and authorities are masters at reversing risk and creating trust. This type of testimonial helps you do just that without the prospect hearing salesy talk from you.

In addition, this type of testimonial also helps you appear more real and more authentic. Do you remember when we talked about having an Authority Character who's real and not perfect, a character who makes mistakes but fixes them? This type of testimonial helps you show off your Authority Character's Heroic Qualities and Dark-Side Tendencies in the best light possible.

Okay, so now that you know what types of testimonials and endorsement you want, the next question becomes: how do you get more testimonials, so you can demonstrate your authority? We'll answer this question in the next chapter.

22

How to Get More Testimonials and Endorsements

On a program of theirs called *The Aladdin Factor*, *Chicken Soup for the Soul Series* creators, Mark Victor Hansen and Jack Canfield, had one rule: you have to ASK to GET. If you don't ask for what you want, you'll rarely or never get what you want. So, the easy answer to getting more testimonials and endorsements is to simply ask your customers and clients. The more complex and insightful answer is that there are three ways to get more testimonials...

1. Ask clients to write you a testimonial
2. Coach clients on what to say
3. Write the testimonial for the client

Ask Clients to Write You a Testimonial

This is how most people get testimonials. And while this method definitely works, it is by far my least favorite way because it's the least effective and the most irritating to clients. First of all, even though your clients want to help you out, they have no idea what to say. So, when you ask them to write a testimonial, they're excited until they sit down to write the testimonial for you. Then, they're stumped and can become aggravated. They honestly want to help you out and give you a great testimonial, but they don't know what to say or how to say it. That's why I prefer to use the other two methods of getting more testimonials. We'll get to those in a moment.

But first, the other issue with this approach is that people are creatures of procrastination. Have you ever procrastinated? Me too. So, do you think your clients are likely to procrastinate at times as well? Of course, they do. If that's the case with the testimonial they're writing for you, then you're either stuck waiting on their testimonial or asking them over and over again for it (i.e. being a royal pain in the arse). I don't know about you, but I hate being a pest to people. Yes, I want their help and their testimonials, but I don't want to seem like a jerk. That doesn't help me. In fact, that starts to erase some of the authority you've built up. So, while this method can work, it's my least favorite.

Now, if you're hell bent on using this method, please understand the nature of the beast and that you'll either have to wait for your testimonial or that you'll most likely receive an "okay" testimonial. Yes, there are times when a client knocks it out of the park for you. But that's the exception, not the rule. So, let's look at methods two and three so you know how to get the best testimonials possible. The next method is…

Coach Clients on What to Say

Like I said a moment ago, your clients want to help you out, but they just don't know what to say or how to say it. So, instead of just asking for a testimonial, you can coach them on what to say. With this method, I like sitting down with my clients or getting on the phone and having a conversation. Of course, before that meeting takes place, you'll want to ask these clients if they're willing to give you a testimonial. Then, after they agree, let them know that one of the easiest ways to give you a testimonial is to sit down and allow you to help them draft the perfect testimonial to make them and you look great. That's a realistic and logical fear of some clients, you know? They're afraid they won't sound professional. That's another reason some clients procrastinate.

In addition to making everyone involved look good and getting a testimonial quickly, helping your clients write the testimonial allows you to get exactly what you're looking for and allows you to help the clients save time. Like I've said, if you've served your clients well, most will be happy to do this. And, they'll be even happier that you're taking the time to help them and not just throwing the job in their laps. Trust me on this, that gesture goes a long way in the eyes of your clients! Plus, this method shows them what a real professional does and how a real authority operates.

The last way to get more testimonials is my all-time favorite way because it speeds up the process tremendously. The third way is to…

Write the Testimonial for the Client

Yep, you can actually write the testimonial you want and have your client sign off on it. Again, this speeds up the process and saves you and them time and possible aggravation. Now, there are two things I want to say about this method. First, there's a trick to making this work, which I'll explain in a moment. But secondly, I want you to know that the second method is more personal, and this third method is more efficient. The second method allows you to speak with your client and craft the testimonial together. Some clients really enjoy that process and will help you develop a better relationship. So, while I love this third method the most because of its efficiency, please understand that the third method not always the best way to get more testimonials. I try to use a blend of methods two and three, depending on the situation, my time, and my relationship with my client.

Okay, with that said, what's the trick to making this method work? The trick is to write at least three testimonials for your client to choose from, and then give your client the option to choose one of the pre-written testimonials or to write you one of his own. Let me explain why this is important. First, giving

> "The right testimonial can dramatically increase your sales, your profits, and your authority."

your client three options allows him to choose the one he's most comfortable with and could imagine himself saying. If you only send one testimonial and he doesn't like it, you'll play email tag with him until he writes the testimonial himself. However, by giving your clients three options, they'll most likely find one that fits with their mindset and what they'd like to say. Always include three to five testimonials for them to choose from.

The second part is just as important. You must also give them the option to write the testimonial themselves. They may not take the option but giving them the option shows them that you want their honest opinion (which you do). Now, I will tell you that I've done this a lot over the years, and I've helped dozens upon dozens of clients get endorsements for their books over the years. Do you know how many times the person asked to choose a testimonial or write a testimonial has written one?

Twice. Yep, only twice in the past eight years has someone wanted to write the testimonial themselves. That's why you must give clients the option. Almost everyone else you ask will simply choose one of the testimonials written for them.

Again, this method saves you time, saves them time, and allows you to get the exact testimonial you want while making them look good and sound professional. This method creates a win-win situation that most clients enjoy participating in.

What If You're Brand New and You Don't Have Any Clients?

If you're brand new and you don't have any clients, then here's what I'd suggestion: I'd consider finding someone you know (maybe a friend, maybe a potential referral partner, maybe someone you know who's a center of influence) and working with him or her at no cost in exchange for a testimonial. Most people will jump at this opportunity if what you do helps them solve a problem or achieve a desired result. Some people hesitate when I bring this tactic up because they want the person to pay for their help. I get it. I truly do. But if you don't have a testimonial and you can't show proof that what you do works for others, then getting clients is going to be a struggle for you.

Now, I'm not saying you should give away your product or service to just anyone or everyone. No, no, no. Think strategically about this. Who could you gift your product or service to that will:

a) most likely get the results you promise,

b) really appreciates the results they'll achieve, and

c) tell other people about the results after they use what you have and write you a testimonial.

Think about these things before giving away your time, energy, and product. The right testimonial can dramatically increase your sales, your profits, and your authority.

23

The Best Type of Referrals

Now, let's explore the second factor to becoming talkable: referrals. Referrals are an integral piece to any marketing plan; however, most business owners don't know how to purposefully increase the number of referrals they get. So, let's start by defining the two types of referrals:

Random Referrals

When a friend refers you to someone he knows out of the blue, that's a random referral. When an associate or colleague refers you to someone she just met, that's a random referral. When a client refers you to someone he was just talking to, that's a random referral. Random referrals happen all the time, and we should be grateful for them. There's nothing sweeter than getting a random phone call from someone who was just referred to you or from a friend who has the contact information of someone who is interested in your services.

The only issue with random referrals is the fact that they're random. You never know when or where they'll come from. So, we can love random referrals, and we can be grateful for them, but we cannot rely on random referrals to sustain our businesses.

Strategic Referrals

Strategic Referrals, on the other hand, are typically more consistent and reliable because, as the name implies, they are strategic and planned out. For example, let's say you own an ice cream store in town, and the theme of your business is based around dogs. You have pictures of dogs on the wall. You have dog treats waiting for the dogs when owners bring these furry friends into see you. You even have dog-bone-shaped sprinkles for human customers. Now, around the corner from your store is a dog grooming business that cuts dogs' hair and nails, washes them, and makes them look fresh and clean. You have the groomers' ideal clients walking into your store every day (literally on a leash), and the groomer has your ideal customers coming in everyday to drop off their dogs.

See where I'm going with this? You and the other owner could come up with a promotion to strategically refer each other business. Maybe a simple coupon exchange is all you need to make this joint venture profitable. You give a dog grooming coupon to every customer of yours for a month, and they do the same for you. Or maybe your venture is more complex, where you and the groomer exchange client lists, segment the lists into best customers, and mail gifts to each other's best customers. Your book, *Mans Best Friends: Dogs and Ice Cream*, would make a great gift for the groomer's clients. Pair your book with a free ice cream and a dog treat, and you're almost guaranteed a visit from the new customer.

That's a strategic referral. You know when to expect referrals, and you may even be able to estimate the number of referrals you'd expect from a promotion like this. The more strategic referral opportunities we set up and plan for, the more predictable our referral marketing efforts become.

Cold, Warm, and Hot Referrals

Now that you know the two types of referrals, let's look at the three temperatures of a referral: Cold, Warm, and Hot.

A Cold Referral is when someone refers you to a potential client who needs help and may be (key words are "may be") interested in what you offer. That's a cold referral. I consider these referrals a smidge better than a cold lead because we gain some credibility from the referrer, but if the referral isn't that interested in our services, then that credibility is wasted.

In contrast, a Warm Referral is when someone refers you to a potential client who needs help and IS interested in what you offer, BUT the referral doesn't know much about you or why he should do business with you.

A Hot Referral is, of course, the best referral temperature because a hot referral is when someone refers you to a potential client who needs YOUR help, IS interested in what YOU offer, and is ready to buy from YOU.

But why are there different temperatures of referrals? There are two reasons. First, intent. A Cold Referral needs help but isn't sold on getting your help or anyone's help. A Warm Referral is interested in what you have to offer but isn't sold on buying from you. A Hot Referral is interested in what you have and wants it from you. The referral must have intent. The stronger the intent the potential client has on solving his problem or achieving his desire, the hotter the referral.

The second reason for the differing temperatures of referrals is your authority position, which is just as important as the reason above because your authority moves the referral from warm to hot. If the referrer has positioned you in the right light, as the go-to guy or gal, as the expert and authority, or as the only person to do business with, then the referral's temperature quickly rises and your likelihood of closing the deal increases dramatically. We're going to talk about this in more detail in a moment, but before we do, we need to know what constitutes a good referral and a great referral.

A good referral is when someone refers us to a prospect who is interested in our solution and is willing to sit down with us or talk on the phone about how we can help him.

A great referral is when someone refers us to a prospect who is interested in our solution, is willing to sit down with us or talk on the phone about how we can help him, and is pre-sold on buying from us.

Now, will we always be able to get good or great referrals from our friends, colleagues, associates, clients, and referral or joint venture partners? Of course not. We're always to going to get random referrals. And we're always going to get cold and warm referrals. That's okay. I'll take those all day, every day because with good marketing and powerful, authority positioning, we can turn those random or cold referrals into closed business.

With that said, naturally, our goal is to increase the number of strategic and hot referrals we get. That's where the real money is: in high-converting, predictable referrals. So, how do we do that? We do that by arming our friends, colleagues, associates, clients, and referral or joint venture partners with the ammunition they need to make the referral-giving process easy and pleasurable. What kind of ammo does the trick? In the next chapter, we'll look at the four pieces of ammunition to help us do just that: make referring us easy and pleasurable.

> We can increase referrals dramatically when we can make the referral giving process easy and pleasurable.

24

Make the Referral Giving Process Easy and Pleasurable

Like I said in the last chapter, while we'll take cold, warm, and random referrals all day long, our goal is to increase the number of strategic and hot referrals we get. In this chapter, we're going to look at how we can do that by arming our friends, colleagues, associates, clients, and referral or joint venture partners with the four pieces of ammunition they need to make the referral giving process easy and pleasurable.

Niching Your Audience

The first piece of ammunition you can use is niching your audience. You see, when you dig down and carve out a niche market for yourself, not only will you have the funds to reach that market and the ability to quickly saturate that market with your message, people will more easily refer to you because they know exactly who makes a great referral for you.

For example, if you're known as the go-to person for helping chiropractors increase their client base, then when I meet a chiropractor I instantly know they're a potential client for you. I don't have to think about whether or not a chiropractor is a good fit for you. I know the opportunity to refer you may arise because that's who you help. You're positioned as that guy or gal. You help chiropractors. Does that mean you can't help anyone else? Of course not. You can. But if people know you specialize in helping chiropractors, then you give their brain a heat-seeking missile to target chiropractors and refer you when the opportunity presents itself.

Personally, for my business of helping entrepreneurs write and publish books, I help a lot of coaches. So, my referral partners tend to send me a lot of coaches as referrals. Can I help other entrepreneurs write and publish their book? Yes. I do that all the time. I love working with education-based entrepreneurs who love to teach their prospects and clients, like speakers, advisors, and consultants, etc. But I make the referral process easy on my referral partners by being positioned as the guy who helps coaches write and publish books. Make sense?

Let me ask you a question: if you were to choose a niche market to make referring you easier, which niche would you choose?

Niching Your Products and Services

The second piece of ammunition you can use is niching your products and services. Yes, not only can you niche your audience, you can also niche your solution. For example, my friend, James Malinchak, did this early in his career when he marketed himself as "that guy who teaches speakers how to make money in the college market." While every other speaker trainer was teaching the same thing to the same market, James stuck out in a sea of competitors by making his speaker training – his solution for speakers – niched to speakers who were interested in making money in an untapped marketplace: the college market.

Again, does that mean you can't help your clients with more than just your specialty? Of course not. But people have a harder time referring you business when you're seen as a generalist. On the other hand, when you're seen as a specialist, an authority on one thing, people remember you, talk about you, and refer you. Think about the medical industry for a moment. When you have a tooth ache, do you see a general practitioner? No, you see a specialist. In this case, a dentist. Now, have you ever gone to the dentist for a tooth ache and they referred you to someone else, like a cosmetic dentist? I have. I went to my dentist a couple years back because one of my back molars was killing me. After I paid him to inspect my tooth, he referred me to a specialist to get my tooth pulled. Why? Because he didn't do that procedure in his office. Instead, he referred me to a friend of his who could take care of me. Someone who specialized in pulling teeth.

From their perspective, do you think it was an easy referral? Heck yeah it was. My general dentist knew the cosmetic dentist specialized in pulling teeth, so when the opportunity came up he only had one guy in mind. You want that kind of specialization for your business too. When a referral opportunity comes up, you want to be the only guy or gal on your friends, colleagues, associates, clients, and referral or joint venture partners mind.

Let me ask you this: from my perspective (in this case, the client's perspective), do you think I was happy getting referred to someone else who specialized in pulling teeth? You bet I was. I didn't want my dentist experimenting on me. I wanted an expert, an authority on pulling teeth. Referrals and clients other people give you should feel the same way, like they're in just the right hands. They don't want to be someone's experiment. They want an authority to handle their issue, solve their problems, or get them to the places they want to go.

Getting Your Audience Fast Results

The third piece of ammunition you can use is getting your audience fast results. Results are king (or queen). Period. So, when you can add value to someone's life by helping him or her get results, word travels fast and your authority spreads like wildfire. Let me give you a couple examples of this nuclear bomb in your arsenal.

A little while back, I went through a period in my life when I didn't want to date anyone; and when I got back into the dating game, I hadn't been on a date in over a decade, so I was quite nervous. So, like any information-seeking entrepreneur, I decided to see if there were any books, CDs, or videos on the subject. What I found was astonishing. There is an entire industry geared towards dating. If you're a busy, male entrepreneur, there's information niched to you. If you're a recently divorced housewife, there's information niched to you. The industry is massive, and while I got a little kick out of all this at first, I came to find out how savvy these dating industry entrepreneurs were.

As this example relates to my original point on helping your target audience get results fast, I found two interesting companies who were using this tactic of getting their clients quick results. The first company was called Double Your Dating, and they had something called "the kiss test." The kiss test description was literally three to four paragraphs long (what some would see as a blog post nowadays), and told men what signs to look for to let them know if a woman was ready to be kissed. Maybe you're laughing because this comes naturally to you, but this company built a million-dollar business using this exact fast-results technique. Some men worry about this social situation. When do I go in for the kiss? Is she into me? Will she reject me? Speaking from experience, these questions are total mind twisters for people in the dating game.

Anyway, I found the kiss test very useful. But I didn't stop there. I found another company, a company that I would eventually buy thousands of dollars' worth of products over a few years' span, that showed guys the first steps on "how to approach a woman for a date." In fact, this company had an entire, a step-by-step system that showed you how to go from approaching a woman and what to say to her, to how to get her number, to how to set up the date, to what to do on the date, and so on. Honestly, from a business owners point of view, these guys knew their stuff and knew how to position themselves as authorities. By the way, if you're interested, that company is called Love Systems.

Now, the point of all this isn't about me and my past dating life. The point is this: when you show your target audience how to get fast results, people talk about you and will refer you to everyone they know. Think about the two examples I just gave you. These two companies did such a great job that I've now used their company names in my book for the world to see. Remember, results rule. What is one idea or one concept you can teach your ideal target audience to help them get results fast? This tactic alone can help you grow your business and get people to refer you more often. This piece of ammunition is that important.

Giving Your Audience the Tools They Need

The fourth and final piece of ammunition you can use is giving your audience the tools they need. This tactic is by far the least utilized referral tactic I know of, but it's the most benefi-

> When you help someone get results, word travels fast and your authority spreads like wildfire.

cial referral tactic you can have in place. So, what do I mean by giving your audience the tools they need? It's simple. Your friends, colleagues, associates, clients, and referral or joint venture partners want to refer you business. If you've niched your audience, then all these referral partners can tell potential referrals about you and how you only work with people like them. If you've niched your products and services, then your partners can tell potential referrals about you and how you have the answer they've been looking for. And if you focus on fast results, then your partners can tell potential referrals about you and how you help people get results fast. These three tactics can help your friends, colleagues, associates, clients, and referral or joint venture partners refer you more business.

However, there's one variable that's remained constant in this equation. Do you see the variable? It's your friends, colleagues, associates, clients, and referral or joint venture partners. The people referring you. Now, we don't want to take these people out of this equation because their referrals trust them. But what if we could give your referral partners some kind of tool or resource to pass along to their referrals so the process moved along faster or made it easier for potential referrals to reach out to you? Do you think that would help you get more referrals? You bet it would.

I learned this tactic almost twenty years ago when I was in the MLM, multi-level marketing, industry. People in this industry have the same issue we do. We want more referrals, but the snag in the process is getting our people to talk about us and refer us. These entrepreneurs need their distributors to refer more business to the MLM company, but the snag in the process is getting their clients to talk about them and refer them. So, how did these MLM entrepreneurs fix that problem? They gave their distributors tools that took the distributor out of the equation, at least at the beginning, so the distributor wouldn't be afraid to talk to people and the referrals would see the company from a bigger level.

To relate this back to the language you've learned so far in this book, the MLM companies created tools (audio cassettes, brochures, etc.) to leverage their authority. That's what you want to do. When you have tools to leverage your authority, you'll make it easier for people to talk about you and refer you, and you'll find yourself getting more referrals as a result.

So, the next question is, "What kinds of tools should you have in your arsenal?" That's easy. The tools you want are the ones that demonstrate your authority. So, if you have a book, then leverage your book. If you have a DVD of one of your speeches, then leverage that DVD. If you have a CD or flash drive where someone is interviewing you, then leverage that CD or flash drive. I'm sure you see the pattern. Whatever tool or tools you have at your disposal that position you as an authority, you want to leverage any or all of those tools to make referring you business easier for your referral partners.

For example, if you're a custom jeweler who designs and fabricates engagements rings, and you've been interviewed about how the mall jewelry stores "rip customers off" by selling inferior products, then you can give your referral partners the audio interview to gift to prospects. The scenario might look something like this:

Weston (talking to a friend): *"Hey man, how long have you and Joy been dating?"*

Friend (prospect): *"We've been dating for four years now. I love that girl. I'm thinking about marrying her."*

Weston: *"Dude, that's awesome! Have you started looking at engagement rings?"*

Friend (prospect): *"Actually, I have. I've been to every store in the area. I just can't figure out which ring she'd like."*

Weston: *"Have you ever thought about getting a custom jeweler to design a ring? That way you get a better-quality ring, and you get exactly what you want."*

Friend (prospect): *"What do you mean, a better-quality ring?"*

Weston: *"I have a friend who's a customer jeweler, and she's always talking about how most jewelry stores sell engagement rings with thinner bands and settings where the diamond can fall out. In fact, I have the interview she recently did. Do you want me to send it to you?"*

Friend (prospect): *"Heck yeah! That would be great. Thanks! But wait. Isn't a custom ring more expensive?"*

Weston: *"Surprisingly, it's not. And she explains that in the interview too."*

Friend (prospect): *"Cool beans. Send me that interview!"*

As you can see from this example, the audio interview (i.e. the tool) makes the referral process easier on me (the referral giver) because I have a tool to leverage. In addition, the tool helps educate the prospect on why he should consider doing business with the customer jeweler while positioning the jeweler as the authority.

Remember, the variable that clogs your referral-getting potential is the human factor. By giving your friends, colleagues, associates, clients, and referral or joint venture partners your authority positioning tools, you're taking the human factor out of the equation at the beginning and making the referral process easier and less scary.

One final note: with Step Four we shifted the focus away from you and looked at how you can become Talkable and profitable with testimonials, endorsement, and referrals. Something we didn't cover that I want to point out is that getting others to talk about you, while important, can be a difficult task. Manufacturing, demonstrating, and leveraging our own authority is easy. Getting others to talk about us – not so much. However, we can succeed and become Talkable if we focus on persistently and consistently adding more value to our prospects, clients, and referral/joint venture partners.

Be Undeniable

We're in the home stretch. You've learned the first four steps in my five-step formula to help you quickly establish trust, confidence, and a powerful, authority position...

Step 1: Be Relevant

Step One is all about *what* you say. It's about being relevant and talking to your ideal, target audience about the situations they're currently experiencing and then showing them that you can help them go from where they are to where they want to be.

Step 2: Be Interesting

Step Two is all about *how* you say what you say. It's

about being interesting, having something interesting to say, and saying things in your own, unique, interesting way.

Step 3: Be Authority-Present

Step Three is all about *where* you say what you say. It's about demonstrating your authority in books, on stages, and in the media, and then leveraging your authority in your office, in your ads, on your website, on your business cards, and anywhere else you can to show your audience you're the real deal and the only person they should do business with.

Step 4: Be Talkable

Step Four is all about *what others say about you*. It's about gathering third-party testimonials and endorsements, leveraging your relationships and getting more referrals, and strategically growing your business with joint ventures and referral partners.

That brings us to the fifth and final step…

Be Undeniable

Step Five is all about *how others see you*. This step is what we're going to cover over the next few chapters. And while this may be last on our list of things to discuss in this book, it's not the least important step. In fact, I'd argue that this step may be the most important of all… at least at first. Why?

Because how others see you is what sets the stage for them to listen to you. If they see you as an authority, then they'll be more open to trusting you and listening to what you have to say. And if they're open to trusting you and listening to you, then they'll be more receptive to buying from you when you prescribe a viable solution to help them conquer their deepest fears, achieve their greatest desires, and move them from the situation they're in to the Promised Land they dream about every day of their lives.

So, to make yourself undeniable, we're first going to explore five ways people judge you before they ever hear you. Then, we're going to look at how you see yourself and the pitfalls with the human psyche. And finally, I'm going to give you a super simple, four-step plan for moving forward after this book, so you can quickly position yourself as an authority and grow your business. Ready? Onward!

25

How Others See You

In this chapter, we're going to look at how others see you. Look, whether we like it or not, how others see us determines if they're willing to listen to us. Judging a book by its cover is human nature. No, snap judgements aren't fair, kind, or right. But they do happen. Evolution hasn't changed this behavior over centuries and millennia, so fighting this nasty habit in the business arena is pointless. So, instead of fighting this unpleasant truth, embrace the fact that people will judge you with the limited information they have.

Now, you may be thinking, "How does embracing this truth help me?" The reason embracing this truth helps you is because while we cannot control how others think or how they see us, we can control what they see and hear, and therefore, we can influence and persuade them to see us how we want them to see us.

In a nutshell, that's what positioning is all about. Positioning is about playing on human psychology and getting people to perceive you a specific way. In our case, we want people to see us as authorities and experts in our field. You've heard me say this over a dozen times in this book: perception is reality. To be seen as an authority, you must do what authorities do, behave how authorities behave, and appear in the same places authorities appear.

However, in this chapter, we need to take a step back and explore the five ways people judge us before they ever hear us. Like I said earlier, if they never hear us, if they never give us a chance, then everything we do to position ourselves as an authority is for not. So, let's dive into the five ways people judge us so we can influence and persuade them to see us how we want them to see us.

Your Title

The words "doctor, author, movie star, CEO, host," etc. mean something to people. For example, have you ever been at an event and you were introduced to the host or hostess of the evening? What immediately goes through your head? Who is this person? What do they do? I wish I could host an event like this. A host is seen as somebody important. His "title" matters.

People are drawn to two types of people. First, people are drawn to authorities. So, when you have a title that positions you as an authority – host, doctor, author, movie star, CEO, etc. – you're seen as an authority. Second, people are also drawn to people like themselves. That's why doctors will answer other doctors' phone calls before they'll answer anyone else's call. That's why parents will listen to other parents about kids and not someone without kids. Sharing the same title with someone gives you affinity with that person and positions you as someone worth listening to.

On the other hand, the lack of an authoritative title positions you poorly and lowers your chances of people listening to you the same way they'd listen to an authority. The second way people judge you is by…

Your Appearance

Your outfit and attire matter. No, you don't have to be the best dressed person in the room. And no, you don't have to spend a bundle of money on your outfits. However, you do have to be dressed for the part you play. For example, when I owned my fitness business, I didn't dress in a suit most days. I dressed the part and wore workout clothing. That was dressing the part.

If authorities in your industry wear a suit, then you should wear a suit. If authorities in your field wear a uniform, then you should wear a uniform. Dressing the part you play so others cannot judge you by your attire is important.

Your accessories matter too. Watches, rings, ties, purses, shoes, etc. all matter. Again, you don't have to spend a fortune on accessories, but being strategic about what you wear

> How others see you determines if they're willing to listen to you.

is smart. People look you up and down before hearing the words you say. So, learning to complete your outfits with some unique and interesting accessories can go a long way. For example, if you wear a suit, wearing a really nice pair of shoes can complete the outfit and make the suit look even more expensive. Sounds crazy, right? But accessorizing is a little trick I learned from a stylist years ago. I remember him saying two things a lot: one, shoes make the outfit; and two, a great pair of shoes makes your outfit look better and more expensive. Now, I don't know if this tip is true or not. But I can tell from personal experience that I've been complimented more times about my outfits since I started wearing better shoes than before I wore better shoes. Coincidence? Probably not.

Now, you may be saying to yourself, "But what if I don't wear a suit?" That's fine. If you're a musician or a fitness trainer or a massage therapist, people don't expect you to wear a suit. That's just an example. Accessories still matter though. So, if you're a massage therapist whose philosophy has an Asian flare, then wearing something like a simple, wooden-beaded bracelet would do the trick. Or if you're in a rock band, then wearing some unique rings would fit your persona perfectly. The point is to have fun with this and look the part you're playing. Again, all these little things add up in your audience's mind and allows their subconscious to paint a picture and perceive you in a specific way.

The next thing we must be aware with our appearance is what we look like. No, I'm not talking about being bald or anything like that. You cannot control those things. I'm balding. I wish I could control that. I can't so there is no point in worrying about it. What I am talking about here is what you can control.

For example, (if you're a guy) when you don't shave, and you look scruffy, that was your choice. You chose to look like that. I'm not knocking looking scruffy. I'm scruffy most days because I hate shaving. But I never go to a meeting or speech like that. Why? Because I can control how I look, and I understand that how I look makes a huge difference in how people see me. Now, if I was in a band or a lumberjack, then looking scruffy may be acceptable. In my environment, looking scruffy is not acceptable. Being clean shaven or having groomed facial hair is acceptable for the part I play. Since I can't grow a full beard (which is sad to me) I go with a clean-shaven look instead.

What about your hair? How does your hair look? Is your hair clean and well-kept or is your hair-do messy and out of control? You can control your hair (if you have hair), so make sure you do something with it.

Do you remember in earlier when I told you about how I studied dating material when I was single? I learned these tips about appearance from that material. The guys on the DVDs and CDs always talked about looking your best and how everything you do that you can control is a choice. Did you leave the house looking frazzled or scruffy? That was your choice. Did you leave the house with a ripped t-shirt and not smelling as fresh as you could? That was your choice. People pick up on these choices and make judgements about you before they speak to you or listen to you.

This appearance stuff may seem to "surface", but keeping up the appearance of an expert and an authority in your field is important. Remember, people have expectations in their heads about how experts look. Dressing the part and appearing that way helps position you as an authority in their minds. I know. I wish appearance wasn't important this way. I honestly prefer to wear sweat pants and tank tops around my house. But if I wore that outfit to an event or speech, I wouldn't be seen as an expert and people wouldn't listen to a word I said. It's sad… but true.

I used to run a marketing meeting where group members learned marketing strategies, and a few, select members of the group chose to upgrade their memberships to the Mastermind level where they would get one-on-one time with me and the other group leader. I remember hosting an event a couple years ago where we gave awards out to a couple Mastermind members. We typically didn't hold our mastermind events the same day as our regular event since both events combined into an eleven hour day. A long day to say the least. So, in anticipation for the long day, all of the Mastermind members dressed casually, mostly in jeans and t-shirts.

Now, why am I telling you this? I'm telling you this because after the regular meeting was over, I had a lawyer come up to me and comment about how unprofessional our Mastermind members looked and how they had no credibility with him. A shitty thing to say? I think so. But this was his perception.

He judged them because of what they wore. Again, I wish this stuff wasn't true, but it is. I didn't survey the group that day, but there's a good chance if he perceived the casually-dressed Mastermind members a certain way then others in the room did too. Appearance matters, so think through how people will see you. Remember, your appearance is your choice.

Where You Appear

The third way people judge us is by where we appear. If people see us on stage, then we're seen as an authority in their minds, and they have a better perception of us. The same goes for our audience seeing us on TV, hearing us on the radio or a podcast, etc. Where we appear matters. But having our name on a book, being on stage, and being in the media aren't the only places we can be. For example, if you're shooting a video, your location says a lot about you and your authority.

So, if you're a rock star, you may consider shooting the video in your studio with lights, instruments, and recording equipment behind. If you're a doctor, you may consider shooting the video in your clean, well-lit office. And if you're a landscape architect, you may consider shooting the video outside, in the middle of a beautiful yard.

Where you do not appear is also important. For example, if you're in the "weight loss" industry, you probably don't want to be caught at the Heart Attack Grille eating a seven-pound cheese burger. That would strip away your credibility pretty fast, don't you think? If you're in the financial industry and teach people how to save money, then appearing at the casino would also be a bad idea. After all, why would I listen to you about money if you're wasting your money on the slot machines?

Who You're Seen With

The fourth way people judge us is by who we're seen with. Whenever possible, we want to be seen with people our audience knows, likes, and trusts. Celebrities are an easy target here because most people are fascinated by celebrities. So, if you can get pictures of you with national celebrities then take that opportunity and leverage those photos wherever you can. Local celebrities are great too.

For example, I live in Pittsburgh and Hines Ward, a retired Pittsburgh Steeler, is a huge local celebrity. Same with Lynn Swann and Franco Harris. Having pictures with these celebs can go a long way if you own a local, Pittsburgh business and you want your audience to see you as someone important.

Of course, celebrities aren't the only option here. You can be seen on TV with local news anchors. Or you can host an event and have a well-known speaker at your event. Or you can have a client who's well-respected in the community. The point here is to be seen with people your audience knows, likes, respects, looks up to, and/or trusts.

Now, the question you may be asking is, "How do you get seen with these types of people?" First, I'd look at your current client base and see if you have anyone like this in your clientele. Then, I'd see who your clients know and ask for referrals to people like this if asking makes sense. Some clients may be nervous about an intro like this, so you can hold a client appreciation event and have them invite the people you'd like to meet. Asking someone to attend an event is easier than asking for a referral. You can take advantage of being the host and get your picture taken with a whole slew of well-known and respected people and/or celebrities. Another option is to look at attending events, seminars, etc. with people like this. With people taking selfies nowadays for their social media feeds, other people are used to jumping in front of a camera without a second thought.

How You Speak

The fifth and final way people judge us is by how we speak. Up to this point, everything we've talked about in this chapter has been about how people judge us *before* we say a word. This last way has to do with when we open our mouths.

Look, before someone listens to the actual words you're saying, he judges you by how you speak. For example, I have a family member (who will remain nameless), who doesn't trust people with an Indian accent because of a business deal that went wrong decades ago. Now, you may think that's terrible. Personally, I don't like that family member's viewpoint or share in his beliefs, but this viewpoint is no different than

> Our goal is to put our best foot forward and get people to look past their prejudices and listen to our words.

disrespecting a slow-talking southerner or not trusting a "fast-talking city slicker." People have prejudices and preconceptions about other people. There's nothing you can do about other people's view. Be aware of a particular audience's viewpoint, so you can choose the best market for you.

Now, like I said before, we don't want to focus on what we can't control. Instead, we want to focus on what we can control. We can control our tone. We can control our pace. We can control the words we use and the intent behind those words. Those are things we can control, and those are factors that can make a big difference in how people see us and if they perceive us as authorities in our field.

So there you are, the five ways people judge you before they listen to you. I want you to remember that some of this stuff isn't fair. It's not right. And it's downright silly at times. But, we can't control how people think and how they judge us. Instead, we want to focus on what we can control: what people see and hear. And because we can control what they see and hear, we can influence and persuade them to see us how we want them to see us.

Also, remember that people have certain expectations in their heads about authorities and what they expect from than authority. So, to be seen as an authority to your audience, you must play this game to win so they see you how you want them to see you. The process of getting others to see us as authorities is no different than you getting dressed up for a night on the town or ready for a date. Our goal is to put our best foot forward and get them to look past their prejudices and listen to our words – because once they do listen, they'll hear relevant, interesting, and unique material that positions you as an authority in their minds and gets them to like you, trust you, and maybe even buy from you.

26

How You See Yourself

How others see you is also a reflection of how you see yourself. In this chapter, we're going to openly explore this hard topic, so you can win without sabotaging your own success. First, let's talk about your authority position. Do you see yourself as an authority in your field? If not, it's okay. Most people don't see themselves this way. However, if you want your audience to see you as an expert and an authority, seeing yourself as such really helps. If your mindset isn't where it needs to be, then there are a several solutions. First…

You Can Fake It Until You Make It

I've been there and done that on numerous occasions. We all have. When I moved from midget football to high school football, I totally faked how I felt. When I was younger, I was one of the biggest kids on the team. Taking charge in the game and demolishing the other players was easy. But when

I moved up into high school football, all of a sudden, I was one of the smallest guys on the team. That was scary. But I couldn't let that stop me. First, that attitude wasn't in my nature. And second, if you ever played football, you know that everyone on the field smells fear, and being afraid makes you a target. So, I had to play through my fears and fake it until the fear was over.

Now, I didn't become the all-star of the team, but I earned a "letter" my freshmen year and started on varsity in both offense and defense every year after that. I'm not saying that to impress you – I'm sure it doesn't. I'm just letting you know that fear is natural and faking our courage until we actually have the courage is what we need to do.

I've done this in the business world too. I remember when I started my first business, a gifts and incentives business, and I had to learn to make a sale. Before that point, I never really made a sale. Sure, I sold myself and my personality to girls I dated. I sold my ideas to friends when I wanted to go somewhere they didn't. We all sell something from the time we start to talk. But I'm talking about going from selling myself and my ideas to sitting in a CEO's office and selling him on my products and services.

In hindsight, the two types of sales are no different from one another. But at the time, the switch was a big, mental leap I had to make. So, I faked it. After a couple of flubs, I started going into the CEO's office like I'd been selling for years. I called them by their first names. I talked to them about their kids. I made jokes. I acted naturally. Was I nervous and scared? You bet I was. But I faked the confidence and ease until they came more naturally to me. I'm sure you've done this at some point in your life. If you don't feel like an authority yet, then you may have to fake it until you feel like a real authority.

Change Your Perspective

The second solution is to change your perspective. I once heard world-renowned, fitness author, Matt Furey, talk about what it means to be an expert. He said, "Experts are people who just know more than the average person. They don't do everything better. They don't know everything there is to know. They don't know more than everyone else in their field. They just know more than the average person."

That description made sense to me and changed my perspective. I believed him then and I still do now. And I can actually confirm his statement from experience. After writing eighteen books prior to this book, I still don't know everything there is to know about my topics. But I know a lot. I know more than most, and I definitely know more than the average person. Knowing more than the average person is what makes me an "expert." That's why I feel comfortable writing about my topics. That's what "gives me the right" to write and publish my own books. I know more than the average person, and I can help average people learn something they didn't know before.

"Head games and mental traps will sabotage your success."

That nugget of wisdom from Matt changed my thinking. And it changed my life. I hope this simple piece of advice helps you change your perspective on being an authority.

Work Hard and Become the Authority

The third solution is to work hard and become the authority. In other words, eliminate any doubt you have by actually being the person you think you are. I remember learning this when I went to college. You see, I was pretty much a straight "B" student in high school. But when I decided to go to college and go into the University of Pittsburgh's pre-med program, I had to make a decision. Was I going to stay a "B" student, or was I going to buckle down and work my ass off to become an "A" student? I decided on the latter and that decision changed my life. Not only did I end my freshmen year of college with a 3.75 GPA, well above where I was in high school, I also learned a very valuable lesson about life. If I wanted to be great at something, I had to study harder than I ever studied before. Becoming an authority is no different. If you want to be great at what you do and have others recognize you as an authority in your field, you must put the work into it, study harder than ever before, and actually become the authority.

Now, like I said at the beginning of this book, you don't have to see yourself as an authority to be seen as an authority. If you simply do what authorities do and behave how authorities behave, your audience will see you as an authority. But sometimes this piece of wisdom is not good enough for some people because their minds play tricks on them. Maybe your mind is playing tricks on you right now. So, even though you're seen as an authority by your audience, you don't see yourself as such. If this is the case, then let me provide you a very simple solution.

Focus on Adding More Value Than Your Audience Expects

Let me ask you this: do you feel that you provide a lot of value to your prospects and clients? Whatever your answer, "yes or no," if you focus on providing more value than your audience expects, then you'll be seen as an authority, and you'll give off the impression that you feel like an authority. It's actually quite amazing how easy it is to trick our brains into thinking or feeling a certain way. When you give, give, give and focus on others, your brain can't focus on how you feel about your authority position.

This is the same trick as smiling in front of a mirror. Have you ever done that experiment before? I learned it from Tony Robbins a long time ago. Go to a mirror and smile for two minutes. I don't mean some little, half-ass grin. I mean smile so big your facial muscles hurt with pleasure. Show all your teeth. Bring the corners of your mouth up to your eyes. Raise your eye brows to the ceiling. Smile big! Go ahead, and try it now.

Did you do it? If so, then you know that a. you feel pretty good right now – yeah, your face may hurt a little, but that's only because you're not used to smiling that big – and b.

nothing else entered your mind during those two minutes. But why is that? When you focus on smiling your brain can't think of anything else. Your brain is putting all its energy into the task at hand. The same goes for when you focus on giving more value than your audience expects. Your brain sees the value you're giving, feels good about all that value, and wants to continue the process.

Okay, there are the four ways to change how you feel about yourself so others see you differently. I hope these strategies help you overcome some of your fears and help you see yourself as an authority if you don't see yourself that way already. I know this process is easier said than done, but don't play head games with yourself. Head games and mental traps will sabotage your success.

So, instead of playing silly, mental games, use these four strategies to help you alter the rules of the game and make winning the game easier. Have you ever played a board game with a child? When my son was younger, I was astonished at how he thought changing the rules mid-game was okay. After all, I was the adult, and we don't do that. We adults play the game the way it's meant to be played. But I let him change the rules anyway because it's just a game, right? Well, you and I play a game every day of our lives with ourselves. But instead of a board game, we play mental and emotional games. So, I pose this question to you: why can't we change the rules and set ourselves up to win the game every time?

Well, we can. And at their core, that's what these four strategies are meant to help you do. They are meant to help you change the rules of your mental and emotional game. They're meant to stop you from self-sabotaging your success. And they're meant to help you see yourself as an authority and win the game of business.

Listen, *you* can win. You *can* succeed. You just have to get out of your own way!

> "I believe there's an inner power that makes winners or losers. And the winners are the ones who really listen to the truth of their hearts."
>
> ~Sylvester Stallone

Your Next Steps...

Knowledge will only take you so far. So, to help you on your journey of becoming an authority and being seen as an authority, I want to give you a four-step plan for moving forward beyond this book...

Step # 1: Become The Authority You Are Meant To Be

Read, watch, and listen to others until you are a real authority in your field. Remember, you don't have to know more than everyone else. You just have to know more than the average person in your target audience. Once you do, then continue to study as you grow your business and really master your craft. Don't stop learning. Don't stop growing. And don't stop giving back to the audience that you best serve. This can be done simultaneously with the rest of these four steps. Simply book time in your calendar to read, watch, and/or listen to something every day for at least 30 minutes. And don't forget to listen to audio books or courses like this one in your car as well as use some of the other things I taught you in Chapter 2 on consuming information faster.

Step # 2: Start Where You Are and Leverage The Authority You Have

If you're not an author, speaker, or media personality yet, then look at what you do have. Do you have testimonials or endorsements? Have you written any articles? Do you have pictures of you with recognized authorities, celebrities, or experts in your field? Whatever you have, start to leverage those things this week. Put your testimonials, pictures, and content everywhere you can: your website, your social media channels, your next ad campaign, etc. Just because you don't have a book or another authority positioning tool doesn't mean you give up. Start where you are, and leverage what you have.

Step # 3: Implement My 5-Step Formula

You can grab your audiences' attention and position yourself as an authority right now by giving your audience relevant information that's interesting and unique. You can keep their attention and start to establish trust and authority by telling your story and becoming more interesting and unique yourself. You can move them from complete strangers to raving fans by showing them more of your Heroic Qualities, showing less of your Dark-Side Tendencies, and letting them into your world by showing them your philosophy. Reread this book and use this book as your guide and implement my five-step formula to position yourself as an authority and leverage your authority to grow your business.

Step # 4: Write a Book

Listen, writing a book will not only immediately position you as an authority in your field, but becoming an author will also allow you to easily create a signature speech that you can become known for. Also, becoming an author will increase your odds of getting into the media. And that's just for starters. A book is the most powerful business tool to ever exist. Nothing else compares to the power and versatility a book brings to you and your business. No other business tool compares, not a business card, not a website, and not a brochure.

That's why I want to help you get started writing your own book. Do you remember in Chapter 15 when I told you that I have a very special bonus for you? I told you that I want to gift you my *Fast Start to Book Writing Success* course that consists of a 32-page manual, six videos, a one-hour-and-forty-minute audio. My *Fast Start* course will help you answer the five, strategic questions you must answer before writing your book. This course sells for $97 on my website, but I want you to have this course absolutely free for reading this book.

All I ask in return is for you to help me spread my message by either gifting this book to a friend or telling your colleagues about *Stop Chasing Prospects*. You may even consider investing in a stack of these books for your clients, mastermind members, or networking buddies (hint, hint, wink, wink, nudge, nudge).

So… are you ready to start writing your own book? You can access my *Fast Start to Book Writing Success* course here: PlugAndPlayPublishing.com/scp-book.

Okay, that's it for now. Thank you for reading this book! I appreciate your trust, confidence, and business. Please follow the four steps I've laid out above, and I'll talk to you again inside my *Fast Start to Book Writing Success* course. See you there!

~Weston Lyon

About the Author

Weston Lyon is the author of nineteen books and one of the only authors to ever write nine books in eleven months (!).

In addition, Weston is the Founder of Plug & Play Publishing: a Pittsburgh-based, authority-positioning company that teaches coaches, consultants, speakers, and other education-based service providers who fear rejection and being treated like low-level sales people how to stop chasing prospects and instead position themselves as authorities in their fields and get prospects to start chasing them by writing a book to grow their businesses.

When Weston is not working, he's enjoying life with his son, family, and friends, training in an array of martial arts, or out on the mountain bike trails.

Are You Looking for a Speaker for Your Next Entrepreneurial Event?

Are you looking for a fun, inspiring speaker who will keep your audience entertained and engaged?

Are you looking for an authority who knows how to thoroughly educate your audience, have them sitting on the edge of their seats, and raving about your event afterwards?

Are you looking for a professional who has given hundreds of speeches, knows what you're looking for, and is easy and fun to work with?

If you answered "YES" to any of these questions, then Weston Lyon is the speaker you've been looking for!

Weston has given over 450 speeches to thousands of business owners and entrepreneurs over the past eighteen years and has shared the stage with fellow, successful entrepreneurs like Dr. Ivan Misner (Founder of BNI & NY Times Best-Selling Author), Michelle R. Donovan (International, Best-

Selling Author), and James Malinchak (Celebrity Entrepreneur who's been featured on the ABC Hit TV Show "Secret Millionaire"), to name a few.

Here's a Small Sampling of What Weston's Audience Members Have Said About Him:

"Weston is everything a speaker should be: fun, inspiring, entertaining, engaging, and educational!"

David Holzer
Owner, Pittsburgh Combat Club

"I've seen over 20 of Weston's talks, and I learn something new and relevant every single time he takes the stage!"

Collin Stover
Author, The Do's & Don'ts of Web Design for Small Business

"Wow, Weston delivered so much high-quality information my head is spinning, and I have pages of notes!"

Dionne Malush
Realty ONE Group Gold Standard

"I want more! Weston was so engaging and entertaining that I felt like he was on stage for less than twenty minutes (meanwhile, he was on stage for almost two hours!)."

Erin Turo
Owner & Office Manager, Turo Family Chiropractic

"Truly inspiring! Weston took a complicated business/marketing issue and broke it down into a simple, manageable solution that I cannot wait to implement!"

Tayon Mitchell
Owner, Engarde Financial Group

Weston has also planned and hosted hundreds of his own live events for entrepreneurs from all walks of life, and he knows what planners need and want.

Here's a Small Sampling of What Other Event Planners/Promoters Have Said About Working with Weston:

"Weston's audiences are riveted! They love him, and I love him!"

Deanna Tucci Schmitt
Executive Director, BNI Western PA

"Your audience will absolutely love Weston's profit-producing content and will be talking about your event for weeks, months, and years to come."

Charlie McDermott
Founder, Turnkey Sales Solutions

"Weston is the easiest, most professional speaker I've ever worked with. From beginning to end (and even after the event), Weston provided impeccable service. I wish all speakers would model after him!"

Becky Auer, $6.5 Million Dollar Woman
Owner, Up a Notch Marketing

In addition to wowing your audience and making your life easier, Weston tailors every speech to your goals and your audience's needs. No two speeches are exactly the same. And every speech is guaranteed to be nothing short of amazing.

To inquire about availability, contact Weston at weston@westonlyon.com or call 412-974-0739.

Made in the USA
Columbia, SC
14 August 2018